Crafting Your Wiccan Path

Connect to Nature, Spirit and Magick Through the Practices of Witchcraft

Sandra Inman

Independently Published

Contents

Disclaimer

Every effort has been made to make this information as complete and accurate as possible. However, there may be mistakes in typography or content.

This Publication is distributed with the understanding that the author is not engaged in rendering professional psychotherapy, psychiatric, health, medical, career or financial advice or services of any kind.

Every person has needs and circumstances that are unique to them and this book does not take those individual needs and circumstances into account.

Questions relevant to the specific professional psychological, psychiatric, health, medical, career and financial needs of the reader should be addressed to practicing members of those professions.

Any person experiencing financial, career concerns, anxiety, depression, stress, health, or relationship issues, should consult with a qualified professional before commencing any new financial plan or transaction, career strategy, change in personal relationships, exercise program, or following any of the teachings, methods, and suggestions described in this book. This book is not a substitute for the reader enlisting qualified professionals to assist with the reader's specific circumstances, issues, and problems.

The purpose of this book is to educate. The author does not warrant that the information contained in this book is fully complete and shall not be responsible for any errors or omissions.

The author shall have neither liability nor responsibility to any person or entity with respect to any loss or damage caused or alleged to be caused directly or indirectly by this book. The book and the contents herein are provided without any warranty, express or implied, as to their effect, completeness, or results received.

Preface

I first heard about Wicca when I was fourteen. I'd always been interested in the "supernatural" and read whatever I could on psychic phenomena, extra sensory perception, astral travelling etc. I am fortunate to have a sister who is five and half years older than me who is also interested in these subjects. She would bring home some great books and I would devour them.

One day she brought home a very interesting book by Justine Glass called "Witchcraft and the Sixth Sense". I loved the book, although I wasn't drawn to the craft at that time. What the book did was introduce me to an understanding of witchcraft that I hadn't come across before. These witches weren't the evil devil worshippers that my Christian upbringing wanted me to believe. Instead, they were people who acknowledged the feminine in the divine and practiced an earth based spiritual tradition.

I never really had a negative view of witches. In my earlier childhood I remember watching reruns of *Bewitched*, somewhat old fashioned now but what I learned from that show was that witches can be good people. I would wish upon the evening star that I could be a witch just like Samantha from *Bewitched*. I guess that wish has come true now, however, as a teenager, I'd lost the incentive. The idea of witches and the term Wicce (feminine of

Wicca) went into the back of my mind where it stayed until the age of 22.

They say that the gods call you when you're ready and often do it in unusual ways. The way for me involved a porch carving on a quaint house that a friend of my mother had up for sale.

As soon as I saw the carving of a women sitting on top of what looked to be a large cauldron, I instantly remembered my sister's book. The word Wicce suddenly came into my consciousness and I felt compelled to find out more.

That same day my sister and I went to a local new age bookstore and there I bought Scott Cunningham's "The truth about Witchcraft Today". I remember it vividly. I couldn't put the book down.

I was hooked. Everything he wrote made sense to me. Each description of the craft as he knew it resonated with me. It felt like I had come home to something that was always a part of me.

It's often difficult to describe this feeling of return. I know many witches feel it. It's as if we have been awakened to our very essence, our soul selves. Coming home is really the only way to describe it.

The connection to nature, the inclusion of the feminine as a part of the divine force and of course the magic, all felt like one big hearty YES!

I was excited. I wanted to know as much about this religion called Wicca as I could know. I wanted to return to myself, my roots, my very being.

So, like most newbie witches, I went on a rampage of book consumption, a feeding frenzy of everything and anything I could find out about witchcraft.

Now this was in the early 1990s. There was no internet,

no Google and no YouTube. The only sources of information were the few books that lined the shelves of a small number of bookstores in my city.

It wasn't easy to find information but I managed. I put everything I'd read into practice. I learned how to set up a circle, cast spells and invoke the Goddess and God.

Still, something was missing. I craved more knowledge. I craved community. I so wanted to know people who also practised this craft. I had a need to share and connect with like-minded people which led me to search for a local coven.

I'd read about covens but I didn't know where to start to look for one. Covens didn't advertise. There was still a lot of prejudice and church groups were very keen to shut anything down that was associated with the occult.

It would take me two years before I found my first coven.

The Coven of the Solar Orb was a training coven that just happened to have a stall at a Body, Mind and Harmony expo in Brisbane where I lived. This expo continues under another name now and is a melting pot of all things new age. It's essentially a spiritual supermarket full of all kinds of therapies, spiritual practices and interesting healing devices.

As soon as I found the Solar Orb's stall, I grabbed hold of their contact details and signed myself up to attend one of their public rituals. I don't remember much about my first ritual with the coven. It was enough to inspire me to join it and attend the weekly training.

We'd meet every Tuesday evening at the high priestesses' house and study Wicca in a rather formal fashion.

We had various types of initiations and participated in creating and performing various roles at Sabbats and full moon gatherings. We'd go camping and perform rites in rain forests and friends' large properties.

I learned so much from those days in the coven. There is nothing better than learning directly from other people. There really is only so much you can learn from a book.

Fast Forward to the current times, I find myself now in the teaching role. It wasn't something I'd planned or even wanted, however, things happen and here I am.

So many people want to learn witchcraft. There is so much information out there. The question I hear the most is "Where do I start"?

When I ask people what they really want from the craft and the practice of Wicca they tell me they want connection.

This connection is often to themselves. So many people feel disconnected. Religious and spiritual paths offer hope. Through the various practices and beliefs people can find a path back to themselves, discovering who they really are underneath the need to please others and fit in with social norms.

They want to connect to nature because they feel so much a part of her already. They are looking at ways to better their lives, become more whole and to be of service to others in meaningful ways.

There is a yearning to connect to the Goddess and the God. They want to feel the support of the deities and not be judged and condemned by them.

Many people are feeling a spiritual disconnect and are searching for a way to connect to the divine. Many people just want to access the divine feminine within themselves and to honour her through everyday practices.

It's not that the divine masculine isn't equally important, it's just that the feminine has been missing for so long that people just want to experience her, pay homage to her and listen to her message. We all have the generative principles of receptive and active energies within us and working with the Goddess and God allows us to awaken these energies and utilise them.

We humans are magickal creatures who are able to participate in the creation process through practicing magic. For many witches the practice of magic connects us to the earth and divinity.

Some of these deeper yearnings are difficult to achieve. A lot depends on how much inner work we do on ourselves.

Often rites and spells aren't enough to help us feel connected to who we really are. A lot of the time negative beliefs and experiences create so much doubt in us that we really feel pinched off no matter what we do.

I hope that this book can guide you toward finding ways to connect to your true Self so that the craft can play a role in helping you become spiritually and emotionally fulfilled.

This book is more than just an overview of what Wicca is and how to practise rituals and spells. It's a guide to help you dig deeper into your spiritual connection with yourself as well as the gods and nature. My aim is to inspire you to practise your craft in ways that bring you a deeper understanding of yourself so that you can create a life of joy, peace and an empowered sense of self.

What was lacking for me for so long was this deeper understanding of myself. It wasn't something my coven could help me with either.

In this book, I hope to inspire you to find the joy and depth in the fundamental rites and practices of Wicca. Many people skim through the practices without really stopping to spend time going deeper. Many hunger for more knowledge and information without exploring the experience through layers of awareness and practise. We start with a seed which through watering and feeding becomes the tree. This takes time, patience and willingness to practise.

Your practice should nourish you and enhance your life for the better. It should bring joy to your heart and help you shine your light in the world. I hope that this book will contribute to helping you achieve the deepest joy and re-connect you with your spiritual essence.

Blessed Be!

Introduction

You can pick up any book on Wicca and immediately gain access to the fundamentals of the practice. These fundamentals don't change, they provide you with a form in which you can create a deep spiritual practice that takes you out of the mundane world and into the realm of your true potential.

The form itself isn't the practice, it's simply a way of containing processes and practices that help you discover and experience the magick contained within. You can think of the form as the Wiccan cup, containing the rich red wine that we consume and hence experience. Each one of us experiences the taste and sensation of this wine differently. The effect this wine has on us is different for each individual too. What I'd like you to gain from reading this book is an understanding of how you can use the Wiccan form to experience the wine of a magical life.

The words in this book are seeds from which you can grow a practice. You'll find the same topics in this book as you would most books about witchcraft and Wicca. These topics never really change, they only become more sacred through exploration and insight.

In Chapter One, I briefly outline the history and philosophy of Wicca. It's through our beliefs and traditional form that we are able to experience the sacred and create lives with meaning and purpose. This chapter touches on karma, the Wiccan rede, ethics, the traditional degree system and my own experiences of these.

You'll be introduced to the Witch's Pyramid and how to create a daily practice in Chapter Two. A simple routine that you can do daily can add so much to your life. Just taking ten to fifteen minutes out of your day to connect with yourself, nature and the gods will change your life.

In Chapter Three, I introduce you to how Wiccans perceive deity. Connecting with the Goddess and God is a very important part of the craft and can often be one of the most difficult aspects for beginners to master. Most people in the west aren't used to working with goddesses and gods so this part of the practice can take time. It's worth every minute of it though. Working with the Goddess and God of Wicca can bring so much joy and fulfillment.

As witches we work with elemental energies and create our own sacred space for ritual and magick. Chapter Four, introduces you to the four elements – Earth, Air, Water and Fire. These forces become a part of our circle work, helping to guard and guide our rites and magick. Our circles are our ritual spaces which we construct ourselves. This chapter will explain what our circles are, why we use them and how we construct them.

Wiccans also use magickal objects such as daggers, cups, pentacles, brooms and cauldrons. In Chapter Five, you'll be introduced to each tool, it's function and how you can use it to enhance your magickal experience.

You can't have a book on witchcraft without including a chapter on magick. In Chapter Six, we'll explore what spells do and how you can achieve the best results with your spell casting.

The lunar cycles play an important role in Wicca. We

work with them for magick and to honour the Goddess. Chapter Seven discusses the importance of the lunar cycle and suggests some tips on how you can easily celebrate the New and Full Moon.

While we honour the moon every month, witches also celebrate the solar cycles and the seasons. We call our solar rites Sabbats and together they make up the eight spoked Wheel of the Year. You will be introduced to the eight seasonal sabbats in Chapter Eight.

When I ask witches what really draws them to the craft, most tell me that it's the feeling of connection to who they really are. This connection is deepened when we engage with self-inquiry and shadow work. The shadow is the name given to those parts of ourselves that we don't want to acknowledge that we have. The work is to uncover these parts, shine a light on them and then integrate them in healthy ways into our understanding of ourselves. This shadow work will be explored in Chapter Nine.

Chapter Ten suggests ways in which you can incorporate sacred dance and voice practises into your witch's craft. Through movement and sound, you can direct your intentions and energy in spell work, honour deities and tap into joyful experiences through your own self-expression.

Finally, in Chapter Eleven, I talk about initiations, covens and where to go from the basic Wiccan practices.

I bring to my current Wiccan practice experiences and processes that I've learned along my path over the last 30 years. Although most of my learning is from Wicca, witchcraft and western occultism, there is a lot that I have learned and incorporated from Buddhist teachers, G I Gurdjieff and Sufi mystics. Even modern-day energy psychology has influenced my practice, especially when it comes to inner enquiry and shadow work.

Regardless of where my influences come from, all of these have a place in my practice. I truly believe from my own experience that Wicca is a spiritual path that can deeply connect you to yourself, nature and the divine.

Why Wicca?

Chapter One

Many people find their way to the craft out of a deep need to feel connected. In the current world in which we live feeling disconnected from other people, nature and ourselves has led to an increase in mental health problems such as anxiety and depression.

So many people feel isolated these days. The Wiccan path offers a way forward, through practices that connect us to nature, spirit and to who we truly are. The problem most new witches often come up against is how to actually practise this craft in a way that brings true joy, peace and an empowered sense of self.

Wicca has a particular form which allows the practitioner to craft a sacred practice that nurtures and develops the soul. We incorporate spiritual rites with magick as a way to honour nature and the divine as well as take initiative and responsibility for our own lives.

Most of the books I found in local bookstores during the 1990s were based upon the Wiccan form of witchcraft. There was a strong emphasis on the Divine Feminine and honouring nature. Authors were very careful to denounce black magic and any association with the Christian devil.

The practice of witchcraft was still illegal in some states in Australia. I personally believe that Wicca helped make witchcraft more accessible and acceptable.

As Wiccans we try to "harm none" and believe that what you send out comes back to you. Many say it returns 3-fold. Whether it does or not isn't the point. I personally don't believe in the 3-fold law, however, I do believe that what we focus on is mirrored back to us.

Call us fluffy bunnies but Wiccans really do aim to be beacons of light in the world, we focus on positive magick and honouring the divine through celebration rather than seeing the world as a place of eternal suffering and torment.

The origins of Wicca's popularity can be traced back to a man named Gerald Gardner. He spent much of his early life in South East Asia and became fascinated with the traditional pagan beliefs and practices of the local people. Gardner also had a strong interest in the occult, was a Freemason and familiar with the works of controversial magician Aleister Crowley.

I remember reading that Gardner wanted to revive the pagan practices of nature worship in northern Europe and in 1954 he published his first book on witchcraft called "Witchcraft Today".

There is much controversy about where Gardner acquired the rituals and practices he attributed to a modern form of witchcraft. Some of it seems to be connected to Freemasonry Aleister Crowley and a revival of northern European pagan practices.

All religions begin somewhere. They all seem to be started by a visionary person who sees a need for change and combines the old and new to create practices for contemporary times.

I believe that Gardner did this. He is alleged to have been initiated into a coven by a woman called Dorothy Clutterbuck. Of course, it's difficult to find any evidence of this as being a witch is something people kept to themselves.

There is no doubt that people were practising witchcraft throughout the ages even when it was illegal. Often it was practised side by side with Christianity or hidden and practised within generations of families.

There are so many books that you can read that reveal the history of Wicca that I'm not going to spend time covering this here.

Gardner founded a coven working closely with a woman called Doreen Valiente. She wrote a lot of the poetry and ritual verses that we still use in Wicca to this day.

It's interesting to note that the word Wicca was rarely used by Gardner. He believed that the word meant "Wise one". Mostly he always referred to himself as a witch.

It is possible that the word derived from an older word Witga which contains "wit" meaning to know but this is something many etymologists are still pondering.

The word Wicca is an old English word which refers to a sorcerer. Wicca is the masculine and Wicce is the feminine. The word was originally pronounced more like "witcha" in old English. The modern word "witch" is derived from this word and took on a derogatory meaning during the Christian reign.

Although Gardner didn't refer to himself as a Wiccan, he referred to practitioners of witchcraft as The Wica.

From Gardner other key people were initiated into the craft such as Alex and Justine Sanders who then hived off and formed their own covens and created their own style of Wicca and witchcraft.

Since the 1960s the word Wicca has become synonymous with modern witchcraft.

In the early days of Wicca and even to this day we are portrayed as nature worshippers. This isn't quite true. We don't worship nature. We connect with nature. We honour nature. We merge with the energy within nature and commune with it and all of its manifestation.

We are accused of being idol worshippers which is also a misconception. Yes, we do work a lot with statues but they are representative of the deities and not the deities themselves. We sometimes call upon a deity to imbue the statute with their energy but we don't worship the statute. The effigies we work with are reminders of who and what we are working with.

We also don't worship our deities, we work with them, connect with them and have a personal relationship with them. Our deities don't need or demand worship.

Wicca is a modern form of pre-Christian European pagan religion. Pre-dating the Abrahamic religions by thousands of years. Consequently, we don't believe in the Abrahamic devil or Satan. In order to worship this devil, one needs to believe in the Christian and Islamic paradigms that contain him. He doesn't feature in paganism.

Wicca isn't a dualistic religion. We don't believe in an ultimate good or ultimate evil that are constantly in battle with each other. Nature does not reflect this. Nature is forever balancing between creation and destruction and without both, life cannot exist or continue.

We understand the hermetic principle of polarity which in some cultures is referred to as Yin and Yang. These poles dance and weave with each other to create existence. The neutralising of these opposing forces is the creation and expression of the Universe. It's a blending of creation and destruction. Neither is inherently good or evil.

Good and evil are human constructs and while they are useful to guide ethics, they don't exist from their own side. The Universe contains all and everything and this includes the aspects of life. Nothing exists in the Universe that doesn't have a function.

It's important to note that just because we don't believe in an ultimate good or evil doesn't mean it's a do what you will regardless of the consequences type of belief. We believe in karma and know that our actions send ripples out into the Universe and that those ripples come back!

Wiccans generally believe that everything is divine and contains the divine. Most of us accept the Wiccan rede, an ethical code which states "An it harm none, do what ye wilt". This means that we try our hardest to not harm anyone or anything, including ourselves.

Wiccans celebrate seasonal rites called Sabbats. We also celebrate the cycles of the Moon which in more contemporary times are called Esbats. We have specific ways of setting up a ritual circle space and special tools that we use for rituals and magick.

It's difficult to pin point what makes Wicca different to the modern western practice of witchcraft. You can certainly see the difference between Wicca and a traditional indigenous religion. However, modern western witchcraft is a combination of various cultures, European occult practices and Wicca.

We live in a global community now. Throughout history religions and practices have morphed and changed due to influences from other cultures. We've never really been isolated from neighbouring communities. We are always integrating and adapting new practices from new places. Witchcraft isn't any different.

Wicca has a distinct northern European flavour as

much of it is derived from Celtic and Norse culture. I have also seen other influences come into the craft over my 30 years of practice. This makes perfect sense to me because people have always learned and borrowed from each other.

Human beings are a social species, we grow through our cultural connections. All cultures and religions have developed through cultural sharing over time. Old cultures disappear and new ones emerge often as hybrids of a fusion of previous cultures merged with the new. This has been going on for millennia.

Witchcraft is an incredibly broad topic. It exists and has existed in pretty much every culture around the world throughout history. It wasn't called witchcraft of course. It was simply a part of the religious beliefs and life of many pre-Abrahamic cultures.

Witchcraft is very practical. It's essentially the art of practising magic. Witches use herbs, candles and all things of the earth to influence change in the world. Through magick, witches can influence minds and events.

There are many different styles or genres of magick. Witchcraft tends to lean toward the type of magick known as sympathetic or folk magic. This style of magick uses objects, symbols or actions which either resemble or are associated with the desired outcome.

A love spell may contain some rose petals sprinkled around a pink candle to symbolise the energy of love or friendship. The candle will be lit and a spell will be recited over the candle. The desired result will usually be visualised in some form as if it has already occurred as the spell is chanted.

In many cultures there would be an individual who

would be responsible for knowing which herbs to use to heal and what incantations to recite to bring rain, a successful hunt or to defeat an enemy tribe. We refer to these people as shamans these days but they were called many different names depending on which culture they belonged to.

One thing they all have in common is a belief in magick and a connection to the world of spirit and nature.

Wiccans share this belief in magick and work to connect to the world of spirit. What defines us as Wiccans though is the form in which we practise and some of the beliefs we have.

Wicca is considered a religion because we believe in deity. Although there are now different forms and styles of Wicca, most of us share a belief that divinity is a combination of feminine and masculine attributes which are expressed through the Goddess and God. Some of us see the Goddess and God expressed through various deities throughout many mythological pantheons.

This can get confusing, especially for people who are new to polytheism and come from a monotheistic background. What can add to the confusion is that some non-Wiccan witches also work with deities while others don't. A lot of traditional witches for example, don't believe in gods and goddesses.

Wiccans also work within a particular form. We cast circles using the elements, we have seasonal celebrations called Sabbats and as mentioned previously, we follow a rede. We honour nature and engage in many of the practices of traditional witchcraft, ceremonial magick and other western occult forms.

It's important to talk more about the "Wiccan rede". It's an ideal and like most ideals or ideologies it's not possible to uphold in reality. Every time we eat, we are harming something. When we pull lettuce out of the ground, we are harming it. Treading upon the ground can mean stepping on some poor insect or grub. Life is a polarity of creation and destruction. We understand that in order to have life we also have to have death. It's how nature works and we honour how she works.

The point of the rede isn't to try to achieve the impossible. It's simply to remind us to be vigilant about how we tread upon the earth. We try to harm as little as we can while living compassionate and fulfilling lives.

This also means that we refrain as much as possible from practising magick that may be harmful to others. This is something that we are often criticised for in the occult community. We simply believe that there are other ways to protect ourselves using magic and to bring peace into our lives without having to go out of our way to cause harm to another person.

We also believe that magick has a mirror like action. What we send out does reflect back to us in some way or another. Many think that this means that if they do harm to someone then the Universe will harm them back. That's not quite how it works, although it can work that way.

Every time we feel the emotional desire to harm, we are actually harming ourselves. Feelings of hatred, revenge and the need for power over another are harmful to us. In sending these thoughts and feelings out into the world we attract situations into our lives that will cause more of these feelings. That's what true karma is.

We live in a world of emotion. Many of us believe that other people are responsible for how we feel. This isn't true. We are the only ones who are responsible for how we feel emotionally. That doesn't give us license to be unnecessarily cruel or to not consider other people's feelings, we simply take responsibility for our own inner world. Someone who curses a lot may not see the negative results in some big way but their emotional life is usually full of anger, resentment and conflict.

It's because of the way Wiccans work with magick and our ethics that often bring us criticism. We are considered fluffy and our practices and beliefs are often seen as empty and inferior to other forms of magical practice. When peace, love and compassion are considered fluff we know we must be on to something!

Many Wiccans are also well educated and practised in ceremonial magick, traditional witchcraft and other magickal and occult practices. This does provide a large degree of eclecticism in the craft.

Traditionally, Wicca had a structured level of priesthood and degrees of initiation. Many covens still adhere to this but many don't anymore. My first coven worked within a degree system but my second coven didn't. It is because of the degree system that Wicca is often criticised for being too structured, formal and even dogmatic.

The three-degree system of Gardnerian Wicca appears to be derived from Freemasonry. With each degree the practitioner would attain certain levels of knowledge and skills. Each initiation would involve a test or "ordeal" which had to be passed in order to graduate to the next level.

The "ordeals" weren't anything scary or dangerous, for example, a common first-degree initiation would be to spend a night out in the forest by oneself. I remember mine clearly, it rained all night. I was drenched. I had a beautiful spot up on a mountain overlooking a valley. I sang songs and talked to the Goddess and myself all night. It was an amazing experience. I loved every soaking wet minute of it.

Over the decades Wicca has changed from its original form. There are now different genres of Wicca. There are Traditional Wiccans, Eclectic Wiccans, Gardnerian Wiccans and Alexandrian Wiccans. There are almost as many different versions of Wiccan now as there are witches. No wonder people get confused. In contemporary times, it can seem that the only difference between a modern Wiccan and a witch is the label they choose to wear.

Wicca really helped people feel more comfortable with witchcraft. Prior to Wicca, witchcraft was associated with devil worship, curses and harmful magick in the minds of most people. Gardner's witchcraft changed that.

Wicca was where it started for me. I never had a problem with its association with positive magic and being benign. I don't see these things as weaknesses. In fact, they're really strengths.

So why Wicca? I like the structure, I like the ethics and I love the form. I love the circle work. I love working with both the Goddess and God. I don't necessarily believe all of the traditional beliefs but I find that having a form helps me give structure to my practice and my life.

I don't put too much emphasis on terms and labels. Being attached to a label such as Wicca or witchcraft defeats the purpose of connecting to our true selves. At the end of the day who we really are has no label. We are simply spiritual beings having an earth experience.

Wicca has changed since the Gardner years. When it was introduced to North America it became influenced by various cultures residing in the United States. American Wicca can look different in subtle ways to Wicca in the

United Kingdom.

I live in Australia and we also have changed the way Wicca is practised. I will talk more about these differences when we get to the chapters on circle casting and how we celebrate the seasonal rites.

To me Wicca is a spiritual practice. We connect to deities, we do rituals and we have beliefs about the spiritual world. Our rites and practices connect us to our own spiritual source as well as to nature and life in general.

What seems to be common among Wiccans is the desire for a sincere connection to nature, the divine and to know our true selves.

Being who we are and being able to express our divine nature is a part of what Wicca can offer. The difficultly is finding ways to access this connection.

So much of this connection comes from the inner work we do on ourselves. Self-exploration and what is called shadow work play a huge role in connecting us to our authentic selves.

Shadow work is the term given to a practice of self-enquiry where we confront our unsavoury personal traits and turn them into productive strengths. It isn't easy work but the rewards are extremely worth the time and effort.

This addition of self-inquiry into Wiccan practices is one of the ways that Wicca moves with the times and becomes a progressive religion.

Even though there are traditional Wiccans who follow in the footsteps of Gardner or the Sanders, many modern Wiccans are eclectic and our practices change with the times. We incorporate new break throughs in epigenetics, energy psychology, natural therapies and quantum physics.

Wicca is not a static or fossilized practice. It is evolving as we humans evolve. It has the potential as any mystical tradition or religion to provide us with a sacred form in which we can deeply connect to ourselves, nature and the divine.

Foundational Practices

Chapter Two

The Witch's Pyramid

Crafting a sacred practice requires us to build a firm foundation. The Witch's Pyramid, also known as the Four Powers of the Sphinx, provides us with the building blocks to help us lay that sacred foundation.

French occultist Eliphas Levi, believed that there were four very important things a student of magick must develop on their path to have any magickal or mystical success. These four powers are TO KNOW, TO DARE, TO WILL and TO BE SILENT (Levi, 1995). Later, magician Aleister Crowley added a fifth power – TO GO.

The first point on the pyramid is TO KNOW. This knowledge comes in many forms. In order to practice the craft, you need to have the knowledge of how to practise. At the beginning much of this knowledge will come from books but often the best way to gain knowledge is learning from other people and putting what you learn into practice.

You'll find that your knowledge of the craft will grow exponentially once you actually start practising. This is where the rubber meets the road. Intellectual knowledge can't bring you happiness but the gnosis that comes from practice can create profound change. Essentially your knowledge will come from books, people and your own experience and insights.

The second point on the pyramid is TO DARE. These points don't necessarily work in any order either. It wasn't too long ago that a person needed to be daring to even read a book on witchcraft or magick to get the knowledge in the first place.

Daring is necessary for you to practise the craft. It's that part of you that has the courage to try new things, stretch your comfort zone and learn from your mistakes.

You need to be daring to practise magick. Witchcraft is still viewed negatively in many places and it takes great courage to go against the norm. Many people don't believe that magick exists. You may also have some fears around practising witchcraft left over from a religious upbringing.

Being daring and finding your courage to try what may seem silly or to do something that may scare you is a part of being a witch. Witches go beyond the mainstream confines and social norms. We think for ourselves. We don't follow the herd. That's one of the reasons why we've been persecuted throughout history.

It takes courage and daring to take back your power. It takes courage and daring to face your own limitations and explore the parts of the yourself you don't like. It takes courage to work on yourself and to become the best version of yourself. It's no walk in the park.

My Gurdjieff teacher used say "the path is sweet". Even in tough times the path is what we make it. Witchcraft is not for the lazy arm chair occultist who sits and reads all day thinking that they know everything once all the books are read.

You need to be daring enough to want a better life. We're often made to feel guilty over wanting more comfort, more security and more control over our lives. In many spiritual circles poverty and going without are seen a righteous. To actually want to have more than we need can seem selfish, greedy and uncaring. This is simply not true. Once you understand magick, you'll know that we all have the ability to create better lives for ourselves. We do have to make the effort though.

It takes courage to commit to learning witchcraft. You will have to spend money, learn new things which may challenge your current belief system and ways of seeing the world.

TO WILL, requires energy to take action and put your knowledge into practice. There will be days when you won't want to turn up for yourself or your craft.

Your will power will be what gets you away from Netflix and to your altar to meditate or do a daily practice. Witchcraft may not come easy to you at first. A witch needs to be able to focus and concentrate for extended periods of time. We have to spend time learning how to manipulate energy and how to combine materials for spell work.

The strength of your will does empower your spell casting. It allows you to focus your intent and connect to the symbols and tools you'll use in your spells. Even if you don't use much in the way of tools, you'll still need to be able to focus your desire. Will has to be cultivated and practised, for many people it doesn't come naturally. In an age of instant gratificationyour will can be incredibly difficult to strengthen.

In occultism, the Will can also refer to your divine Will. The divine Will is not the wilfulness of the ego. The divine Will is of a higher vibration. It is not an invitation to do what you please regardless of the consequences. The divine Will comes from a much higher source.

The next point on the Pyramid is TO BE SILENT. This

silence has many meanings. It is tradition to keep silent about magickal practices. One of the reasons is to avoid the negativity of other people influencing your magick. Often friends and family may be sceptical or even jealous of your success so it's better to keep your spells to yourself.

Some practices may challenge other people's beliefs. There are many folks who just aren't ready for magickal knowledge. It may even be physically dangerous for you to "come out" about what you do. Magick has hundreds of years of secrecy in its past for good reason.

Being silent also means exploring your inner world through meditation and contemplation. By quieting the mind, you can access your intuition and learn more about yourself. When it comes to scrying, divination and spell work, your ability to focus your mind becomes extremely important.

The last point is TO GO. We live in the material Universe so we have to take our knowledge, daring, will and inner listening out into the world and actively create our lives. It's about being in the world and taking action to help the spells manifest.

Magick needs to move through the physical plane. It will most often manifest through an action or event. It may inspire you to make a phone call or take a different route on your way to work.

Magick is rarely miraculous. Sometimes miracles do happen but most of the time you will need to take mundane everyday action to allow the magick to manifest. You can't just sit back in an armchair and expect money to fall from the sky.

You can practise applying these powers to your daily life through developing a daily practice.

Creating A Daily Practice

A daily practice is the first step toward bringing your practice out from the books and into your life. It's about turning up for yourself every day even if it's for just a few minutes. Creating a sacred routine everyday helps you to ground yourself, gets you in touch with you and helps you establish that connection to your craft, yourself and the Goddess and God.

The meaning, the depth and the feeling of connection will develop over time as your practice evolve and grows with you. The first place to start is to commit to turning up for yourself every day.

Your witchcraft practice is yours. It's something that you can fine tune to suit your life, your personality and your lifestyle. It provides a means for you to take time out of your busy day and relax, focus and connect.

The more you experience this connection to your true being the smoother your life becomes. Even during the difficult times you'll find that a daily practice will keep your rooted to your spirituality giving you the strength and resilience you'll need during those hard times.

The more you connect to the Goddess and God the easier it will be to connect with them when you need their help and assistance. It's a way of knowing that you're not alone.

Once you've committed to this practice you can start by creating a sacred space.

Sacred spaces vary from person to person. Many people create a sacred space in the corner of their bedroom while others only have their bed. Some will be able to allocate an entire room to their practice.

As far as a daily practice is concerned you really only need yourself. Once you get used to doing it, you'll be able to create sacred space wherever you go.

Grounding

I like to start my practice by connecting to the earth. Try focusing on the connection of your body where it touches the ground and imagine that you have energetic tree roots reaching down far into the earth's core.

It is through these roots that you can later draw up energy into your body to help you create a sacred space using the energy from the earth and from the space around you.

You can do this either seated on a chair or cross legged on the floor. Take three deep breaths in and out to settle your mind and then focus on where your body contacts the ground.

Imagine tree roots reaching down into the earth from either your feet or tail bone. Feel the heaviness of the earth beneath you. Soon you will draw energy up this pathway into your body and then project it out into the space around you.

This kind of grounding is great for bringing a sense of peace and relaxation. Often, we are so much in our heads that once we begin to ground through our bodies, we feel a tremendous release of tension and anxiety.

This may be the only thing you do as your daily practice in the beginning. That's Ok. It's a practice. It gets you connecting to the earth, concentrating and tuning in to your senses.

Projecting a Sphere of Light

To make the space sacred it's as simple as projecting positive energy around your body. This can be done quite simply by drawing from the Universal energy field and from the Earth into your body and then projecting it out and around you.

There is a powerful magnetic field emanating from the heart. According the research conducted by the Heart-Math Institute, your heart generates the largest magnetic field in your body. In fact, the magnetic field of the heart is 60 times greater in amplitude than the brain's field when recorded on an electroencephalogram (EEG). Research has shown that when two people touch or are in close proximity to each other electromagnetic energy is exchanged between them (Braden 2014).

Studies are showing that the heart's magnetic field contains information or coding that is transmitted outside of the body. It seems that emotions influence this information and when we change our emotions, we also change the coding.

The information contained in this field has the ability to affect people and animals around us. So, it makes sense that it can also be used to create a sacred field around us too.

You can imagine a golden or blue light starting in your heart area and with each breath out it grows larger and larger. To help you grow this space around you, keep drawing the energy up through your energetic roots up your spine and then allow that energy to shine through the heart area.

You can do this practice anywhere. I often do it in my car when tail gaiters get too close. It actually repels them back to a safe distance.

The grounding and the heart shining exercise doesn't have to take long once you get used to it. They can be done within 1 minute.

Connecting to the Goddess and God

You may want to then connect with the Goddess and

God or perhaps just one of them. This is simply a matter of calling on them to be present with you. If you are naturally psychic you may feel their presence if not then just imagine they are standing before you.

You may find that you prefer to work with a particular goddess or god. That's fine, call them in and imagine they are in front of you. Feel into what that feels like. Allow your imagination to run with this at first. Over time you'll find that images will spontaneously occur without you having to create them.

In the next chapter, I'll be sharing with you more about how you can connect with the Wiccan deities and you can incorporate these techniques into your daily practice.

Developing Awareness

At this point in your practice, you may want to touch base with how you're feeling physically and emotionally. Your body plays a very important part in your life, it's the vehicle you travel through life in and it's important to keep it healthy and strong.

During your daily practice you can tune into your body and observe how you feel emotionally too. Our emotions are our guidance system and if you are feeling any unpleasant emotions, you can take this time to learn more about what they may be telling you.

You can also take this time out to journal. Spend five minutes writing down your thoughts without taking your pen off the page. Don't edit what you're writing, don't check spelling or correct mistakes. Allow your subconscious mind to communicate with you so that you can get insight into your thoughts and feelings. You can use these for future shadow work sessions.

Meditation

One of the most important daily practices of all is meditation. I know it doesn't sound particularly magical and witchy but it really lays the foundation for success in rituals, magick, divination and connecting with the gods.

There are many forms of meditation and different forms work better for different people. The type of meditation that I recommend is a simple mindfulness meditation whereby you just concentrate on your breath in and out, in and out beginning with two minutes and working your way up to 15 minutes if you can.

It's natural for your thoughts to wander during meditation. The important thing is that when you notice this wandering simply focus on your breathing again. Keep bringing the mind home to the breath.

There are a couple of things that you can add to this process depending on whether you're visually, auditory or kinaesthetically orientated.

If you're visual, light a candle and concentrate on the flame while focusing on your breathing.

If you are auditory, you can focus on the sounds around you without becoming distracted by them. It's even better if you can meditate near the ocean, a waterfall or somewhere where there are natural sounds. Simply listen to the sound while gently focusing on your breathing.

If you are a body person or kinaesthetic then focus on being in your body while you meditate. Feel the floor or cushion under your backside and sense your body in space and the space around your body. Do this while also focusing on your breathing.

These extra sensory stimulants help the mind concentrate and provide a focus to help you bring the mind back to when it starts to go swinging from thought to thought which it will do.

sure that you are physically comfortable while ing. You can sit on the floor with your legs crossed and your back straight or if that's not comfortable or practical, sit in a chair with you back supported in an upright and aligned position.

The goal with this kind of meditation is to quiet the mind and relax the body. You will find that this will help increase your ability to concentrate which will make it easier for you to focus on your rituals and spell work for a longer period of time.

Of course, you don't have to do all of these steps every day if it's too much but you'll notice what a difference it makes in your life by practising every day.

If you are wanting to learn a simple daily practice then a good place to start is with my simple five-day course called *"The Ultimate Guide to Starting a Wiccan Practice that Works"*. You can access this course by going to: https://tinyurl.com/DailyWiccan

This course takes you step by step through simple practices you can do to help you ground, create sacred space, connect with deities, meditate and even work simple magickal intentions into your day.

Creating a daily practice may seem like a big step to take as it will require you to add new things to your daily activities. You may be tempted to leave it until tomorrow but we know that tomorrow never comes. A good question to ask yourself is "Where will I be 6 months from now if I do nothing?"

One of my teachers used to say, "Try it and see, don't try it and see". What could happen if you started your practice today? What will happen if you don't?

The Goddess and God

Chapter Three

It took me a long time to fully understand the concept of the divine as being expressed as a Goddess and God. Having come from a Catholic background, I'd come to understand the divine as a single masculine creator. Even though a nun once told me that God was both male and female, I couldn't get past the "he" pronoun meaning masculine. Why call it he if it's both or neither?

Language informs us. It describes things. Using he to refer to God implies God is male. I think most people who have grown up in an Abrahamic religion associate their god with being masculine in nature.

When I first discovered the divine feminine, it felt like I'd rediscovered some hidden truth. I spent a long time only relating to the divine as the Goddess. It wasn't that I didn't acknowledge the divine masculine it's just that I felt the need for a divine mother in my life. Sometimes we go to opposite extremes in an attempt to find balance. Essentially, I was swapping the "he" for a "she". I related to her as mother. It filled the gap that was left from years of God the father.

Discovering the divine feminine was liberating in so many ways. It enabled me to embrace the unique power of the feminine. It helped me embrace my sexuality and not feel that it was somehow bad or evil. It helped me stand in my power as a woman. It also helped me understand and accept the differences between the masculine and feminine energies.

When we stop seeing the masculine and feminine as opponents in battle with each other, when we stop competing with each other, we can learn to appreciate our differences and acknowledge what we have in common. The masculine and feminine are a binary but not a polarity. They complement each other and also are a part of the unity of all things, like concentric circles.

In occultism, binaries combine to form a ternary in order for creation to continue. The ternary is made up of the two binaries but is in itself a third force. When we acknowledge the Goddess and God within ourselves and the world, we become the third force. From our divine masculine and feminine aspects, we can create what we came here to create. As I've explored the feminine in the divine as well as in myself, I've actually come to understand and respect the masculine more and hence the God of the witches.

Wicca is often referred to as a duotheistic religion and many Wiccans work with the Triple Goddess and Horned God. Wicca is also polytheistic. Many of us work with different goddesses and gods.

When I was in my first coven, we worked with deities from various pantheons but always referred to them as the Goddess or the God. This can get confusing. We used to say that all goddesses are one goddess and all gods are one god. They are like the facets of a crystal. The divine feminine has many facets or aspects as does the divine masculine. Together they make up The One or The All. This is the Unity of all things often expressed as divine consciousness of which we are also a part.

The goddesses and gods may present as individuals, yet they can also dwell within us as we resonate with their energy and connect with their essence. We are a part of them and they are a part of us. In the realm of spirit there can be a lot of paradox whereby something is both one way and its opposite at the same time. Confusing, yes, but some things just can't be explained logically, they really have to be experienced.

In the beginning of Wicca, the Goddess always seemed to take precedence over the God. When Wicca became popular in the USA many feminist covens emerged who followed the Goddess and completely omitted the God.

For a long time, I worked with the Goddess. I didn't refer to her by any name other than mother or "the Goddess". I felt that she was an amalgam of all of the goddesses throughout history and culture. I still feel this. It's an all and everything approach. One and many at the same time.

Traditionally, the Goddess represents the feminine aspect of divinity or the force of life present in all manifest things. She is the great mother being expressed in the earth itself, the stars and the moon. She is the receptive aspect or magnetic force. Where the Goddess is the All Mother, the God is the All Father and it's through this principle of gender that life is created.

The principle of gender is a hermetic principle much like the Taoist Yin and Yang. The word gender comes from a Latin root meaning to procreate, generate or to beget. The Hermetic principle doesn't refer to physical sex or reproductive organs. A quote from the Kybalion expresses it very clearly: *"Gender is in everything; everything has it's male and female principles, Gender manifests in all places"* (The Kybalion, p48).

The God is seen as the masculine aspect present in animals, the sun and the active aspects of energy and life. He is the great father being expressed as the sky itself, the winds and the sun. He is the projective aspect or electrical force.

The concept of the triple goddess demonstrates the cycles of life, beginnings, peaks and decline represented by the maiden, mother and crone. These aspects are seen in the waxing, full and waning cycle of the moon. She is respected as the giver of life, the one who gives form to life and also the destroyer of it.

The God manifests through many aspects as well. He is the horned god, vegetation god, lord of the beasts, the green man and lord of the harvest. Whereas, the Goddess is represented as a triplicity, the god is often dualistic. This is the tale of the Oak and Holly king, an agricultural story of growth, death and rebirth of the land.

The Oak King rules the waxing year while the Holly King rules the waning year. They battle each other at the solstices. The defeated king withdraws to return at the next solstice to win once more.

There are other myths also associated with the theme of the dying and resurrected god found in myths all over the world. Here, the God is born of the Goddess at the winter solstice and grows throughout the waxing half of the year, reaches his peak at the summer solstice and then begins to wane until his death at the winter solstice only to be reborn once again.

As the triple goddess is reflected in the cycles of the moon, the god is associated with the waxing and waning of the solar year.

Many Wiccans also work with individual gods and goddesses. These deities usually rule over specific aspects of nature and life. There are gods and goddesses who reign over storms, fertility, prosperity and love. Most deities have more than one attribute and they often synchronise with other deities from different pantheons.

Beyond the many deities most witches acknowledge a unifying force which runs through and underlies all things including the deities themselves. Some call this Qi, Mana, Prana, Megin and Spirit. The gods and goddesses lend their flavour to this energy and invite us to work with them to connect more deeply to this energy and to help us utilise it to make change in the world through magick.

Many witches experience deities differently. Some see them as purely psychological, as archetypes which dwell within the human psyche. This is a very popular way of working with the deities, especially in the more main-stream new age circles. This is often referred to as the psychological model. Many people will talk about connecting with their inner Aphrodite or Inner Athena when they are oscillating between exploring love and also being assertive in the world.

Most Wiccans experience the deities as entities in and of themselves. They can exist as a part of us due to the connectivity of the universe, yet are also self-governing energies existing in their own right just as we do. This is referred to as the entity model.

From an animistic point of view the deities are the aspects of nature that they govern, for example, Zeus is the rain as much as he is associated with influencing it. When we connect with nature, even by touching the rain we are connecting with his essence and with the energy that makes up all things. When we touch the rain, we are connecting physically with Zeus himself.

There doesn't have to be conflict over these two models. You don't have to choose one over the other. They exist together. The Goddess and God are within all of us as they are also expressions of a unified consciousness. Connecting with the deities is really the only way for you to get to know them and what they are. A book cannot do this.

When we channel a deity two things happen. We have the possibility of perceiving their energy and communicating with them and we also filter a lot of this perception through our own bias. Our bias contains our world view, ideologies, ingrained beliefs and of course our own ego. These filters can distort and colour our interpretation of the information we are receiving.

This is why people of different belief systems give very different information about the world of deity. One person will perceive a deity one way and another may contradict this. Hekate is an example of such a deity. To some, she is a dark goddess often representing the harmful aspects of nature, yet she is a Goddess who walks all worlds and has very enlightening, compassionate and liberating qualities about her.

This does make it difficult when we try to perceive how much of our connection is indeed just our imagination and ego fancy and how much is direct communication. This is where the term "Know Thyself" becomes so important. When we know ourselves, shadow and all, we are more likely to be able to determine what is divine revelation and what may be just our beliefs and egoic fantasies.

When I teach the craft, I do show students how to work with various gods and goddesses as well as tap into the students own spiritual self. Through the experience of working with different deities the witch begins to experience the different energy of each manifestation of the divine feminine and masculine.

My first connection with a particular goddess actually occurred when I started to study Buddhism. Buddhists have amazing meditation practices and I found that their philosophy about non-attachment incredibly helpful. While learning about Buddhism, I became familiar with their main female deity Tara. She has 21 aspects, many of which correspond to various goddesses from Greek, Celtic and Egyptian pantheons.

She was the first goddess I connected with and worked with in any great depth. I turned to her when in distress and when elated. She became my go to goddess for many years. You'll find that there will be particular goddesses and/or gods that you naturally gravitate toward. Sometimes, it's like they have picked you to work with them.

Through Buddhism, I was introduced to mantra. A mantra is a combination of seed syllables that are linked to the deity you are working with. Mantras have a number of advantages. They can help with concentration. If you find meditation difficult then a mantra can help you quiet your mind and give you something to focus on at the same time. Mantras also connect us with the deities themselves. When we vibrate the sounds, we resonate with their vibration. This vibratory aspect also makes mantras perfect for raising energy for spells and healing work.

Over the last couple of years, I've been working closely with Hekate. She is a goddess whom I never expected to work with. I'd been working with the God for a couple of months and I just happened to be looking at the waxing moon one day and the thought occurred to me to establish a connection with the Goddess again. At that moment a thought about Hekate entered my mind and I heard, "it's time to work with me now".

A couple of days later an email appeared in my inbox regarding a course especially dedicated to working with Hekate. For some reason I felt I had to sign up and I did. Since then, I've been working with Hekate every day. It's not surprising that she made herself known to me when she did. Just as I was about to launch into formally teaching witchcraft, she shows up. She is known as the Queen of the Witches after all.

My daily practice involves setting up a sacred space, invoking and chanting to Hekate. I've also worked with other deities during this time as well but not on a daily basis. The connection is very much heart felt. I feel their presence as I say their names and call upon them. I give them small offerings of either food, drink, energy or oils.

People ask me how to connect with the deities. Actually, it isn't difficult. The only thing to watch out for is that you need to be discerning enough to know when you are truly receiving communion with them and when it's just the ego making things up.

If you are unfamiliar with connecting to a goddess or god it's not that difficult to establish a connection. Imagine they are standing before you. If you are invoking the Goddess and God together, see yourself standing with them in a triangle. Each one of you is a point in the triangle. Energy connects the three of you.

Beginning with the imagination doesn't mean it's all make believe. At first it can be difficult to feel anything. It takes practice. Some people who are particularly good as perceiving energy and presence may be able to connect the first time they try, others will have to wait.

Light a candle, stand with your feet firmly on the ground. Feel the ground under your feet. Feel that connection to what supports you. It may help you to visualise an image of the Goddess at this point. She may be a statue you have seen, a painting or your own impression. Then call upon the Goddess by saying something like this:

> *I call upon the Great Goddess of the witches,*
> *I call upon the one who is many,*
> *I call upon the lady of the moon, the seas and*
> *the earth,*
> *I call out to the mother of all things,*
> *Be with me now, wonderous lady of the Wicca,*
> *Be with me now as I celebrate the love and light*
> *which you bestow upon us.*

Take a moment to feel into the Goddess' presence and then call upon the God.

> *I call upon the God of the witches,*
> *I call upon the one who is many,*
> *I call upon the Lord of the hunt, of forests*
> *and animals,*
> *I call out to the father of all things,*
> *Be with me now, wild lord of the Wicca,*
> *Be with me now as I celebrate the strength*
> *and courage which you bestow upon us.*

After you have connected to the deities, focus on what you feel. Write about it in your journal.

Connecting with the deities is incredibly fulfilling and truly a magical experience. This is why I allocate five modules in the Mystery Witch School 101 Academy to working with various deities. So many people feel alone and disconnected, working with the deities fills a void and enriches our lives beyond what we can imagine.

Crafting Sacred Space

Chapter Four

People from all around the world create beautiful buildings and perform special rites and ceremonies in order to experience the sacred. In times past, people have laboured long and hard to build beautiful churches, synagogues and various types of temples globally. From a magickal point of view, these edifices do contain energy that is built up from hundreds of years of millions of people performing sacred practices.

As Wiccans, we tend to create sacred spaces in our homes and gardens rather than large public buildings. To Wiccans, nature is a sacred space and most of our rites are celebrated outdoors in forests, atop mountains and on beaches.

When we create our sacred space, we slowly raise the vibration of the area we are working in. This space becomes a haven and a refuge of clear light that helps to raise us out of the mundane cares and troubles of the world. This slow transition allows us to transform our consciousness from the mundane to the sublime.

One of the things I teach at the Mystery Witch School is how to transition from the mundane world to the peace within. What you're creating is the space where you can connect to yourself, to the universe and to the gods. It's like you're entering into another reality.

We experience a change of emotional energy when we walk into a sacred space. Time seems to slow down and the cares of the mundane world often dissipate.

Wiccan Circles

Energy oscillates in circular pulses and Wiccans tune into these pulses in order to utilise the energy during rites and magical workings. One of the ways that witches work with these pulses of energy is by creating a sacred circle.

Circles symbolise completion and continuity. The circle is complete in and of itself, you can't determine where it begins or where it ends. It's a symbol of wholeness and unity. Wiccans believe that life exists beyond what we experience as physical life. Life in the form of consciousness exists beyond the physical mundane world.

A circle represents the continuity of consciousness. Most Wiccans believe in reincarnation which is a continuity of existence. We know from science that energy always exists. We also know that an atom is made up of 99% energy. If our physical bodies are made of atoms then we too are 99% energy. This energy can be changed and transformed continuously. If this recycling happens in the mundane than why would it be different from a spiritual perspective? It makes sense to us that there is more to our existence than this one physical life.

While energy may change form, it's still energy. Energy moves in a vortex, any energy work that we do will oscillate and vibrate in a vortex. For example, the oscillations of energy coming from the palms of the hands of reiki practitioners show increased speed compared to the energy coming from a person without healing or reiki attunement.

Nature is full of spiral patterns and cycles. Even the

way the wind and air currents move around the planet are circular and cyclical. The Wiccan wheel of the year is a cyclical progression of the yearly seasons. Every year the earth circles the sun. As the earth progresses through this cycle, we experience seasonal changes from winter through spring through summer through autumn and back to winter again.

The Four Elements

Before I explain how a traditional Wiccan circle is created, I need to briefly introduce you to the four elements.

The four classical elements play an important role in many magickal traditions. These elements are Earth, Air, Water and Fire. They were believed by the ancient Greeks to be responsible for the creation and destruction of matter. Although western chemistry has many more elements on the elemental chart, these classical four are still worked with in magick and mysticism.

In western magick, these elements are considered to be spiritual energies that reside in physical and spiritual forms. There are many various spirit beings who are associated with each of the elements and it's really a matter of choice as to which ones you work with.

The easiest way to connect with these energies is through nature. The earth provides very clear representations of the four elements. On a physical level each of the elements are made up of qualities of moisture and temperature. For example, earth is cool and dry, water is cool and moist, air is warm and moist and fire is warm and dry. Each of these elements is associated with one of the four directions and this is where it can get complicated.

Western magick was developed in the northern hemisphere in the middle eastern area so the elements were

associated with the natural occurrence of their
equivalent. Earth was in the north because it is cold
further north you get. Fire was in the south because it
is where the sun is the strongest at the equator. The largest water source was to the west and the sun rises each
morning in the east bringing in fresh morning air.

In the northern hemisphere, this way of working with
the elements is pretty standard. In the southern hemisphere the north and south are usually reversed due to
the positioning of the equator and the south pole. This
means that the element of earth will be associated with
the south and fire with the north.

These elements help us create a sacred space as well as
protect it from any malevolent energies or entities that
may wish to disrupt the circle. There are many different
entities associated with the four elements. In Western
magick sylphs personify and govern the element of air,
undines are associated with water, salamanders personify fire and gnomes govern earth.

Within my first coven we also worked with archangels -
Raphael governs the element of air, Michael governs fire,
Gabriel governs water and Urial governs earth. It's not
unusual for Wiccans to work with angels. We see them as
just another type of spirit. In traditional Wicca the spirits
and Angels who guard the four directions are known as
the watchtowers.

Spending time connecting with the elements themselves allows you to feel the lifeforce of the earth. Each
element expresses itself in nature. Fire is felt through the
heat of the sun and the warmth of flames. To experience
the fire element within you take notice of your body temperature. Place your hand on your forehead and feel into
the warmth of your body.

Earth is experienced as the weight beneath our feet. If you go outside and stand barefoot upon the earth for three minutes a day you can begin to balance the earth element in your body and connect to its grounding energy.

When you swim or bathe you experience the fluid element of water. Drinking water can help you connect to this element. As you drink a glass of water focus on feelings of gratitude, abundance and health. Your intentions influence the physical structure of the water. Feel the cool liquid filling your body while cleansing and nourishing it.

A fresh wind that invigorates you is the force of the element of air. You experience the element of air all of the time through your breath. Spending a few minutes throughout the day just noticing the feeling of the air as you breathe in and out can attune you to the element of air.

To better connect to the elements, pick one to focus on each day. Throughout the day take notice of how that element appears in your life and environment.

Meditation on the elements will give you more depth of understanding of their energy and power. You will begin to experience how the elements work within you too. Sometimes, you may feel that you have too much fire and need to balance this with the element of water.

Too much of an element can manifest via emotional and physical symptoms, for example, too much heat can cause headaches and migraines, too much water or damp can cause congestion. Balancing these is beyond the scope of this book, however, you can start by tuning into your body to see which elements may be out of balance.

Wiccan Circles and the Hemispheres

Wicca as we know it today began in the United Kingdom. When you read anything about Wicca you will see a lot of northern hemisphere associations and imagery. This includes animal symbols, the plants and the order of the Sabbats.

If you live elsewhere in the world like the southern hemisphere you can feel a little bit out of place. Even if you live in the northern hemisphere but live closer to the equator it's still going to feel different. The animals will be different, the herbs will be different and the climate isn't going to really sync in with the typical Sabbat associations and imagery.

So, what do you do when you are working within an earth-based religion and the usual books and information don't compliment where you live?

From an earth-based point of view the Sun appears to be traveling in an arc from east to west across the sky. In the southern hemisphere it arcs toward the north and in the northern hemisphere it arcs toward the south. Basically, it arcs toward the equator.

Of course, we know that the sun isn't the one doing the travelling but from our position on earth it appears this way. When doing magick or astrology we always work from a geocentric point of view.

You will come across the words deosil and widdershins in your Wiccan travels. Deosil means sunwise and widdershins means anti-sunwise. In the southern hemisphere deosil is actually anti-clockwise. This is because the sun arcs in an anti-clockwise direction from east to north and then to the west.

In the northern hemisphere deosil is clockwise. This is because the sun arcs in a clockwise direction from east towards the south and then to west. Some people confuse the meanings thinking that deosil means clockwise whilst widdershins means anti-clockwise. This is not the case. The ancients connected to the movement of the sun and not clocks.

There is also another reason why we circle differently in the southern hemisphere and that's because of the Coriolis effect. If you're in the northern hemisphere and you go and flush your toilet you will notice that the water will actually spiral downwards in a clockwise direction.

Flush the dunny in the southern hemisphere and you'll experience the water spiralling in the opposite direction – anti-clockwise.

If you look at a weather map, you'll notice that the highs and lows are also opposite between hemispheres.

Highs in the northern hemisphere move clockwise whereas in the southern hemisphere they move anti-clockwise.

So, the sun, the winds and the currents move in opposition between hemispheres. The moon even looks different when she waxes and wanes. As an earth-based practice, we have to take notice of these differences and work with them.

Some solitary witches place the elements according to where they live much like the early civilisations did. They may have the ocean in the east and get the cold gusty winds coming from the west. In this case they will place water in the east and air in the west.

How to Create a Wiccan Circle

The most common form of Wiccan circle is one where we cleanse and consecrate the space using a besom, salt water and incense. We then call in the elements and invoke the Goddess and God.

To begin, the floor is swept with a besom or broom. This is purely a cleansing action. This broom never touches the actual ground. It sweeps out energy not physical dirt.

The sweeping action is often done in a circular fashion. Essentially what you're doing is sweeping all of the negative energy out of the space. If you're working in a room, you will sweep the energy out the door.

Consecration

Next, we consecrate the space in order to make it sacred. Essentially, it's a statement to all of the spirits out there that this is sacred ground. It's also telling yourself that this is a sacred space. This allows you to psychologically and energetically tune in to your purpose and tune out the cares and concerns of the mundane world.

When we consecrate our circle, we work with the four elements. We blend the water and earth using water and salt.

As we bless the water we say:

I bless and consecrate this creature of water so that it will be helpful to me in my work. Remove all malefic and replace with benefic.

As we bless the salt we say:

I bless this creature of earth so that it will be helpful to me in my work. Remove all malefic and replace with benefic.

We then pour the salt into the water and sprinkle the mixture around the circumference of the circle making sure to travel deosil.

Next, we light incense to represent fire and air and walk around the circle cleansing and consecrating the space with the smoke.

At this point further consecration and cleansing occurs

when you walk around the circle and project energy out toward the circumference of the circle either with your athame, wand or your own hand. This energetically marks the boundary of the circle, banishes negative phantasms and sets it up as a protected, sacred space.

I personally see this energy as a blue ray of light similar to a laser. I imagine it coming up through my body from the ground and through the pores of my skin and projecting out through my Athame or fingers (if I'm not using my dagger).

It's important to note that consecrating a space is not necessarily going to protect that space from all negative influences. However, if you use the same space over time, it will develop a higher vibration which will deter many negative energies.

You can regularly consecrate your space if you are working in a place where there is negative energy. These energies may come from people or psychic disturbances. Whether it's the people you live with or just the neighbourhood, regular consecration of your space will help lift the vibe.

When creating a Wiccan circle, we go one step further with protection. It is here that we call in the four Watchtowers or Quarters. Via this action we are requesting the assistance of the elemental spirits to protect the circle from all malevolent beings that could potentially come from each of the four directions.

Wiccans vary in the way we evoke the elements. Traditionally we used pentagrams to evoke each element, however, in modern times many witches simply visualise the element and call it forth without the use of a pentagram.

While I teach the use of pentagrams in the Mystery

Witch School, I will show you the simpler ve.
out the pentagram in the book.

The order in which you call in the elements
different depending on whether you are in the no ..iern
or southern hemisphere. A simple way to do this is below.

Stand with your arms raised in a welcoming gesture.

For the Northern Hemisphere

Beginning in the East, call upon the element of Air. As
you do imagine the sound of the wind swirling before
you.

*All hail and welcome to the element of Air in the East. I call
you to attend and guard this circle giving it the breath of life!*

Walk toward the South, call upon the element of Fire. As
You do imagine a fire before you.

*All hail and welcome to the element of Fire in the South. I
call you to attend and guard this circle and give it warmth!*

Walk toward the West, call upon the element of Water.
As you do imagine a flowing waterfall before you.

*All hail and welcome to the element of Water in the West. I
call you to attend and guard this circle and wash it clean!*

Walk toward the North, call upon the element of Earth.
As you do imagine the weight of the earth beneath your
feet.

*All hail and welcome to the element of Earth in the North.
I call you to attend and guard this circle and build it in*

.rength!

For the Southern Hemisphere

Beginning in the East, call upon the element of Air. As you do imagine the sound of the wind swirling before you.

All hail and welcome to the element of Air in the East. I call you to attend and guard this circle giving it the breath of life!

Walk toward the North, call upon the element of Fire. As You do imagine a fire before you.

All hail and welcome to the element of Fire in the North. I call you to attend and guard this circle and give it warmth!

Walk toward the West, call upon the element of Water. As you do imagine a flowing waterfall before you.

All hail and welcome to the element of Water in the West. I call you to attend and guard this circle and wash it clean!

Walk toward the South, call upon the element of Earth. As you do imagine the weight of the earth beneath your feet.

All hail and welcome to the element of Earth in the South. I call you to attend and guard this circle and build it in strength!

Once we have cast the circle, we then invoke the Goddess and God and continue with our rite or magical work. Try this example below:

In this sacred place I call upon the Ancient Ones. Great God-dess, Lady of the moon, seas and land. Great God, Lord of the Sun, the animals and the hunt. I ask that you bless this space and myself as you are honoured this night.

When we're in a Wiccan circle with other people and begin to dance or move around the circle, we build a vortex of energy. The energy is especially powerful when working as a group.

A single person can dance around a small circle and also generate a lot of energy, however, the energy increases exponentially when there is more than one person. This energy can be used for spell work or to simply raise the vibration of the area you're working in.

To close down the circle, we say farewell to the elements. Some witches will move around the circle in widder-shins to farewell the elements in the reverse order to how they were evoked while others don't. In my coven we continued to move deosil around the circle and farewelled the elements in the same order as we evoked them.

Sometimes it not practical to set up a full circle like the one just described. You may find that you only want to set up a circle for spells, sabbats and lunar rites. Sometimes the simple practice of creating a circle of light as described in the daily practice is all you need.

As you experience setting up sacred space, whether it's a full circle or just your daily circle of light, you'll begin to notice a change of energy. You may find that other people will comment on how the energy of your space has changed.

When you get used to creating sacred space, you'll also improve your perception of energy in general. You may not be able to describe what it is but you'll know when you walk into a space whether that space has a good vibe or not.

Take note of how you know it too. Where do you feel it?

Generally sacred space is something you're going to notice from a bodily point of view. You're going to feel safer. You're going to feel more peaceful and you're going to notice that the temperature has warmed up a bit. Contrast that with being in a space that has a lower vibrational energy and you'll notice a difference. Such a space may feel heavy, you may feel ruffled and the temperature may be cooler or just plain cold.

Take notice of how those two spaces feel and compare the differences. The more you do this the easier it will become to tune in more to what a sacred space feels like.

So, when you're doing your circle work or daily circle of light, take a moment to connect to what that space feels like to you. Write down three things about this feeling that's different to how you felt before you set up your circle.

My experience

In my experience there are three main things that I notice when I'm in consecrated space. The first one is a change in temperature. As soon as the circle goes up or I project a circle of light around me I feel warmer. This happens even when doing a sabbat circle at Yule when it's cold. Once the circle goes up, the temperature rises as well. It can get quite cosy.

The second thing I notice is a sense of peacefulness. When I've been in circles with other people and we've completed the ritual and farewelled the elements we will remain standing in the circle space for some time. We don't want to leave it. It just feels so peaceful. It's almost like time has stood still or slowed down.

We realise that we are all a part of something much bigger or grander than ourselves. We become aware of how inclusive the Universe actually is of everything and everyone in it. It is truly a magickal and mystical experience.

If you're doing rites in the same space over time, you'll notice that the area will develop a peaceful feeling. This feeling will increase and remain for longer periods the more often you perform the circle work. Over time the space can transport you automatically to a higher vibe and more peaceful state of being. If energy has been deliberately raised in the space through dance or mantra then it is vibrating even more!

A sacred space can grow from a very mundane environment if ritual practices are constantly being performed. This is one way you can make your own home or room a sacred space.

The third thing that I've noticed about a sacred space is that I feel safer in them. I've been in environments where the energies or local spirits felt quite suspicious of us. Once the circle was cast the energy transformed and we felt supported. I feel that the spirits didn't take kindly to humans but once they knew that we were honouring the sacred, they became quite welcoming.

Whenever I do a rite in nature away from my home, I always welcome the local spirits of the land and ask their permission to do the rite. They usually will participate and lend their energies to protect us during our stay.

When creating a circle, we are working with beings and energies beyond ourselves and mundane existence. We get to connect to the forces of life and become transported to another state of being in the world. Life opens up and we are no longer stuck in the confines of physical existence. Over time we come to realise that we are players in a much larger cosmic show.

Tools of the Trade

Chapter Five

Although magick and ritual can be practised without the need for objects, tools such as a dagger, pentacle, wand and cup add a special vibe to the work, plus, they do hold energy which we can use in rites and spell casting.

Wiccans use many tools for magic, directing energy, offerings and working with the four elements. There is quite a list too:

Pentacle – Five-pointed star in a circle
Cup – a goblet or chalice
Athame – Dagger with black handle
Wand – Wooden wand
Altar – Small table
Besom - Broom
Cauldron – Cooking pot or potjie
Scourge - whip
Sword – Double edged
Boline – sickle shaped knife with a white handle

These tools have various practical and magical functions. Many of them help us channel the energy of the associated element into our rites and magick. Other tools have more practical and energetic functions. Every time you use your tools you are building a stronger relationship with them.

When we use our tools over a period of time, they start to contain our energy. They become extensions of ourselves. This can be compared to a musician and their musical instrument. When a violinist picks up their violin, they connect with it as if it is a part of their own body. The instrument picks up their energy adding subtle nuances to the music each time it's played.

Your tools are no different. When you place your spell candle on your pentacle each time you perform a spell then your pentacle is going to accumulate magical energy.

Magick is all about energy. Sometimes we want to perform a rite or spell but our energy just isn't as strong or as focused as we would like it. Connecting to your tools can help you tune into the right frequency and help you tap into the energy needed to complete the rite.

Your tools will also contribute to whatever ritual or magic that you're doing once they've built up that energy through regular use.

Wiccan tools can differ from tradition to tradition. Depending on what tradition you're in will determine what tools you use and what they are associated with. What follows are some of the main tools.

The Pentacle

The pentacle can be made out of copper, wood or ceramic materials. It is essentially a circular object, a circle on the outside with a five-pointed star on the inside.

When the single point of the pentagram is facing upwards it symbolises spirit and the other four points below it symbolises the four elements. This upright pentagram demonstrates how we master the base elements in order to connect with our essential spiritual nature and will. When upright it is typically considered an evolutionary pentagram

If the single point of the pentagram is facing wards with the four points above it, it can symbolise how the elements are dominating the will of the practitioner. This pentagram is often used to symbolise dark magic. It's not so much that it's evil, it's more about our earthy desires and attachments being dominant over our will. This is what is called in occultism an involutionary pentagram.

The inverted pentagram can be used to represent shadow work. Through shadow work we explore how our conditioning and attachments to our worldly desires can dominate our true selves. This form of inner inquiry helps us see where we become disempowered so we are no longer slaves to our unconscious desires and beliefs. When our higher Self becomes the master of our ego we line up with the upright pentagram.

Our higher Will is not the wilfulness of the ego either. It is the will of our higher spiritual consciousness. It's the part of ourselves that is not attached to earthly desires or gains.

As a tool, the pentagram is a symbol of the element of earth and manifestation. We use our pentagram to bring our will into the manifest world. As a feminine symbol it gives form to what we have created on an astral level through our thoughts and feelings.

When doing spell work you can place your spell materials, amulets and talismans on your pentacle to ground and earth the energy. Through this action you are ritually earthing your desire into the physical realm.

Your pentacle can be used as a magickal shield too. If you are warding off energy you can hold your pentacle up as a shield while doing protection magick. You can also se this method to deflect any negative energy that may be directed toward you back to its origin. This is one of the reasons Wiccans often use a pentagram as an amulet. It has the power of protection and deflection.

Many witches wear a pentacle or pentagram around their neck as a necklace or hang one over their front door for protection. This protection can be from ordinary people, spirits or psychic attacks.

You can also carry your pentacle with you to connect more to its energy and the earth element. Each time you see your pentacle, you will be subconsciously connected with the elemental energies of the earth. Try meditating on your pentacle to help you attune more to the earth element. Take it with you on excursions into nature. You can even bury it for a few days in the earth to help attune it to the elemental energy.

The Cup

The cup symbolises the element of water and is associated with the feminine. This tool is more receptive in nature as it contains and gives form to whatever is placed in it.

Fill a cup with water. Notice how the cup gives the water shape and form. How could we benefit from the rain if there were no rivers or containers to capture it?

As a symbol of the element of water, the cup nurtures and nourishes via the contents that it contains. Of course, the cup could also contain substances that poison and destroy too but that's not what Wiccans use our cups for.

The element of water inspires flow, surrender and receptivity. As a receptive tool the cup reminds us that we have to be open to receive our magickal intent. We have to surrender to how the magick wants to work.

Going with the flow is as important to magick as willing

our intent is. When we are inspired, we have to gi
to the inspiration in order for our idea to manif
physical way. Ideas are pretty useless until they are contained and take form. The cup represents this aspect.

In rituals, the cup is filled with wine and either offered
to the deities or shared around the circle in a coven. As the
cup is shared among conveners, it becomes a symbol of
generosity, community and sustenance.

The cup can contain other beverages as well. For example, at the seasonal rite of Imbolc the cup may contain
beer to offer to the Goddess Brigid. The cup could contain
milk for a full moon rite or if you're doing a daily practice,
it may contain water.

When we bless the contents of the cup, we are creating
something sacred. We're also showing gratitude for what
we have and for what we can share with each other.
Working with the cup helps us remember to practise appreciation for the abundance of food and water that the
earth provides. We are nothing without the earth, other
people and our connection to spirit. The cup reminds us
of how dependent we are on others which is quite humbling.

Your cup can also be used to bless objects and people. If
you're working with crystals that are water friendly you
can charge them up with the blessed water in your cup.
Simply fill your cup with water, bless the water and then
dip your crystal in the water. Remember, not all crystals
can tolerate water so do your research before you do this.

You can use this verse to consecrate your cup.

*"I consecrate you oh creature of water, remove all things
malevolent. Cleanse and purify this crystal so that it may
serve me in my work"*

Of course, your cup can be used to help you connect to the element of water. Simply hold the cup in your hands and meditate on the image of it filling and overflowing with water.

The Athame

A favourite tool among witches is the Athame or dagger. Traditionally, it is a double sided black handled knife. The athame is only used to direct energy and to cut through energetic space. It is not used to cut flesh or to kill or to draw blood.

When it comes to the athame, the first thing you will learn is how to direct energy. We use it in this fashion when casting a circle and using the athame to draw an energetic ring around the circumference. Many Wiccans also use it to draw the pentagrams at the four quarters when invoking the watchtowers using the pentagram method.

Essentially, it's an extension of your own energy or Qi. Wherever you're pointing your dagger is where the energy is going be focused. Think of a laser beam and your athame as the laser.

Traditionally, the athame has a black handle but I've seen modern-day ones that can deviate from that. Some athames are made from copper, iron and even obsidian these days, however, it is tradition to use steel. The power comes from you and not the blade. You channel your energy through the dagger. This means that you need to be able to channel and project energy. The type of metal will influence the energy though, so do some research to discover which metal may work best for you.

If you are familiar with reiki or hands on healing, you'll know how to do this. I teach a lot of energy work at Mys-

tery Witch School. First you start by projectin
out from your palms or fingers and then you lea
the same via the athame. It's important to know how to
channel the universal energy from the earth and around
you so that you aren't using your own energy. You don't
want to deplete yourself. The grounding exercises in your
daily practice will help you draw in this energy so that
you can then direct it through your athame.

Once you draw the energy up from the earth imagine it
flowing down your arm and through the dagger. You can
imagine electric blue light emanating from the tip of the
blade out to the circle edge. This is something that you
can practise.

The athame is closely related to the sword and shares
the same symbolism. The sword is as a symbol of truth
which cuts through the veil of lies, the blade cuts both
ways. The double edge reminds us of the principle of polarity - for every positive there is always a negative.

Double edged swords also cut through deception so that
you can see what is behind the veil of secrecy. This clearing action is also used to help you clear the space of
any unwanted energy, transforming baneful energy into
more positive energy.

The dagger can also act like a key to unlock wisdom. As
a symbol of the element of air, it is associated with the intellect, mind and communication.

Athames are great to use for banishing. If you are
cleansing a talisman or charm you can clear away any unwanted energy before you bless and consecrate it. This is
especially useful if you're using second hand objects and
you want to remove the previous owner's energy.

Use your athame for shadow work. This isn't a traditional use of an athame but it is very effective. Write

down on a piece of paper any beliefs that you have about yourself that you no longer want or no longer serve you. Take your athame and rip it through the paper. This is the only time that you would use your athame to actually cut through something. What you're doing is symbolically cutting away that thought or belief.

To connect with the element, move your athame through space in short sharp actions as if cutting away an invisible curtain. Listen to the sound of the blade as it cuts through the air. Move it fast then try cutting the air slowly. Feel how focused this action is. Try to sense the air around you as you cut through it.

The Wand

The wand is featured in folklore, myths and fairy tales as a magical item that can do wonders. Many people believe that the wand contains all of the magickal power and in fiction it does, however, in reality it is simply a tool that witches and magicians use to command authority and sometimes draw in energy.

You can use your wand to help you stand in your magical power. Once it's been consecrated and charged, it will accumulate energy each time you use it. Simply holding your wand in your dominant hand can help you feel more empowered.

The wand is generally made from wood and wood comes from trees. Trees are rooted in the earth so they connect with the underworld, they also have a trunk and branches that reach toward the heavens. When we hold our wand, we become like the tree. A tree symbolises the connection of earth and sky and if you're looking at the earth as mother and the sky as father you've also got that balance of the feminine and masculine energies.

The wand is a symbol of fire. The fire energy is the in-

spiration from the mental realm which needs to b᠎
nelled into a receiving device and given form. Th
the wand we draw down the inspiration from the hea. ...
down toward ourselves and into what we want to manifest. That's why we use it to invoke the Goddess and God
or in some forms of magick to command spirits.

Some witches even cast their circles using the wand
rather than their athame. In this case they are channel-
ling energy through the wand from themselves out into
the world. Generally, it's more about calling or bringing
something in rather than directing energy outward.

You can also use the wand as a defence because you can
draw in protection around you as opposed to banishing it
as you would using your Athame.

Different trees have different magickal attributes and
when choosing the wood for your wand you'll want to
consider these. Wands are often made from oak or birch
trees, however, you can do your research to find out what
trees grow in your local area and work with a wand more
attuned to the energies of the land where you'll be doing
most of your magick.

The wand is a masculine tool associated with fire. You
can think of gathering fiery energy with your wand and
using your cup to distribute the energy. This way you're
using the binary of masculine and feminine principles to
harness creative energy which becomes the third principle. This third principle balances and harmonises the
binaries.

To connect to the element of fire using your wand simply imagine that your wand is a fire stick and feel the
power of fire. How does the roar of the flame sound? How
does it inspire you?

How to Consecrate Your Tools

Before you start using your tools you'll want to cleanse and consecrate them. This can be as simple as running them through incense smoke or sprinkling them with consecrated water. Cleansing your tools will clear them of any extraneous energy from their manufacture and handling by other people prior to you obtaining them. Consecrating your tools makes them sacred objects and prepares them for use in your craft.

As you're slowly running your tool through the smoke imagine all of the negative energy simply dissolving and being cleared away. Imagine the smoke is absorbing any unwanted energy and transforming it into neutral energy. As you run it through the smoke all you need to say is:

"I cleanse and consecrate this wand so that may it may be useful to me in my work, remove all malefic and replace with benefic."

See it as being clean and purified ready for you to put your energies into it. This process doesn't have to take long. A minute spent feeling into alchemical transformation is all you need.

Once you've cleansed your tools, you'll want to put your energy into them so that they become an extension of you. The simple way to do that is place your tool between the palms of your hand and project your energy into it.

Traditionally, various colours are associated with the each of the four elements. They are listed below:

Wand - Fire - Red
Athame - Air - Yellow
Cup – Water - Blue
Pentacle – Earth – Green or Black

You may also visualise or feel into the energy of the element your tool represents. See your wand being surrounded by flames. Your athame can be surrounded by the yellow colour of air. Visualise your cup being immersed in water and your pentacle grounded within the earth.

Once you're done you can start using your Wiccan tools for any ritual or magick of your choice.

You need to make sure that no one else uses your tools. You don't want other people's energy blending with your own. So don't lend your tools to others or put them anywhere where curious people may want to pick them up and look at them.

The Besom (Witch's Broom)

The broom has been associated with witches since the Middle Ages. We use it mostly for clearing away unwanted energy from a space, however, historically, it does have other symbolism associated with it.

In pagan practices throughout Europe the broom held a place as a symbol of fertility. It was used in marriage ceremonies to encourage successful procreation. The couple would ride the broomstick in the same way children ride a hobby horse.

This riding of the broom was also used to stimulate the fertility of the land herself during various rites and seasonal celebrations. Broom riding was also used in conjunction with the use of hallucinogens. This is where flying on the broomstick most likely originates

The broom is a masculine and a feminine symbol. The handle is the masculine aspect due to its phallic shape and the brush and cap are feminine. It's easy to see the sexual symbolism here. Traditionally, the handle is made from ash and the brush is made from birch which was tied together with willow.

When making a broom yourself you can use whatever natural materials you have available to you. It's good to use trees that are local to where you live. The energy of the materials your broom is made from can subtly influence your broom's energy. They give it a personal touch and character.

Small besoms can be used in spell work to symbolise creation and new life energies. As the broom symbolises the fusion of male and female aspects it has a very creative energy. In this case you would lay your besom over a symbol of your desire, chant your incantation over it while visualising your magic taking effect.

The broom is most often used to cleanse a room or a space to prepare it for ritual. In this case the broom sweeps the air and never touches the ground.

You can use the boom to energetically cleanse your home. This energetic sweep will remove negative energy. Always begin a home cleansing by starting at the back door and sweeping through every room as you move toward the front door.

To store your broom, you can hang it over your front doorway with the bristles facing downward. Doing this protects your home by preventing any negative energy from crossing the threshold. You can also place your broom under your bed to protect you as your sleep.

If you work in an office, you can create a small broom, charge it up and keep it on your desk. Many people won't even notice it's there and if they do it will look more like an ornament.

You can also carry a small broom with you for protection and even place one in your purse or wallet.

The Cauldron

Cauldrons have been associated with witches for a very long time. Mainly used for cooking, they are used by modern witches to create brews and burn herbs. Traditionally, the cauldron was used to create herbal potions and for brewing beer.

Traditionally, the cauldron should be made from iron which is known as the menstrual blood of the earth. The cauldron is a container in the same way that the cup is so it is also a feminine tool. Many of the attributes of the cup also apply to the cauldron.

The cauldron gives shape and form to your spells. It receives the energy of your will. You can project energy into the cauldron to enchant its contents.

You can also use your cauldron for scrying. Fill it with water and place the cauldron against a dark background, place yourself into a meditative state and as you focus on the dark water, look through it as if you're trying to see what is underneath the cauldron. Take notice of what thoughts and images fill your mind.

For spell work you can burn petitions, cleanse and charge crystals and burn your candles in it as a fire proof container.

When I use the cauldron in group work, I will sometimes place flowers in it, divination stones or use it to burn petitions. My old coven used to burn a small fire in the cauldron. This was the fire we would jump over during the Beltane fire rituals.

Cauldrons come in different sizes. In most new age or witchy stores, you'll probably find rather small cauldrons that are good for burning herbs. If you're wanting a larger pot then a less costly way to obtain one would be to buy one from a store that sells South African Potjies.

Your iron cauldron will need to be seasoned with cooking oil especially if you're going to be cooking. Rust is something that will build up in your cauldron if you don't regularly cure it.

If you do get some rust, you can always scrape this off and use it for black salt. This powder is used to absorb negative energy by combining it with sea salt and sprinkling it in an area that you want to cleanse.

The Altar

That altar is a microcosm of the sacred space. It's a symbol of unity where all of your spells, tools and rites come together.

As a central hub of energy, your altar will accumulate energy every time you use it. Many Wiccans will have permanent altars set up on side tables and ledges. I have a square altar that I can move around and another altar that is stationary. Altars can be as simple and temporary as a coffee table or even a desk draw.

On this altar you will arrange your sacred objects and any spell materials and ritual decorations depending on what you're doing at the time. Many people have a permanent altar set up for specific deities or even ancestors.

Even though an altar isn't necessary it does serve a number of purposes. It's a storage for your ritual items. Your altar helps your centre your attention into one unified area.

Altars also provide you with a sense of connection to your craft. Via your altar you connect to your practice. Your altar will also help you connect to the four directions and to the God and Goddess as they will have a place on your altar. Regular use of your altar will empower it with energy which makes it a potent hub for magick and spell work.

The Scourge

The scourge isn't used so much anymore. We never used one in any of the covens I was in. It's mostly associated in Gardnerian Wicca. It's essentially a symbol of suffering and sacrifice. The magickal path isn't an easy path and often involves sacrifices. These sacrifices are usually time and energy but as small as these sacrifices may seem they can feel like suffering at the time.

The Boline

Traditionally the Boline was a small curved knife with a white handle. It is used for cutting herbs and plants to make potions or to use in spell work. Many use the boline to inscribe sigils onto candles.

While various Wiccan traditions also use other tools, the ones mentioned above are the most common. Use your tools as a way to connect with your craft. They are sacred objects and by simply using them you can feel more connected to your practice.

Witchcraft and Magick

Chapter Six

When I think back to what attracted me to the magickal path, I have to say that it was the ability to be able to influence my life in the way that I choose.

I think most people come to magick looking for a sense of having more control over their lives. That doesn't mean we are control freaks, we just want to feel we have a say in what goes on. So many of us feel like jellyfish being tossed around by the ocean tides, magick gives us a sense of being able to actively craft our life.

There are many definitions of magick. It's difficult to pin it down because there is no scientific way to explain it. It simply appears to be the ability to influence events and people through the focus of our will.

Magick seems to work by combining focused intention, we project our desire out into the Universe, take appropriate action in the world to allow the magick to line up the events and people needed to bring the result to fruition.

Magick isn't some supernatural phenomena, instead it's completely natural. The Universe is reflecting back to us what we are putting out. Like a feedback loop. This ability to influence such change seems to be a part of the human condition. Our ancestors were performing magickal operations way back in the stone age.

The popular notion of the law of attraction describes it

this way – what we think about the most, we will receive. This is pretty scary given that a lot of the time we are focused on things we don't actually want.

Magick workers aren't as cynical about manifesting every thought like some people in the Law of Attraction movement are. We do understand though that our thoughts and words are very powerful when there is a strong desire and emotion behind them.

The use of magick allows us to navigate our way through life in a way that makes it more bearable and enjoyable. Magick enables us to co-create with all of the other people and beings who are co-creating as well. It's very unifying. Essentially, magick connects us to All and Everything in the Universe.

While most of us become attracted to magick for egoic reasons we soon learn that it is more than just fulfilling the desires of our materialistic whims. Magick gives us the ability to align our life to our highest will. Magick is creative. It's as if you are actively creating your own computer game while you're in the game.

We are very powerful beings and we've been disempowered by a lot of manipulation and brainwashing throughout our history, however, we are becoming more conscious of our abilities and magick is now becoming a part of mainstream culture.

Now people, who in the past, would never have practised magic are practising it under the guise of manifestation or law of attraction. They are creating vision boards and writing manifestation lists in a more rudimentary and simpler way to how witches practise spell crafting.

People are starting to wake up to our inability to be able to take an active role in our lives. Magick does empower us and through spell crafting we have the means to create our lives in a more harmonious fashion.

Magick isn't all about control. To practise magick completely we have to work with the masculine and feminine energies of will and reception. We project our will into the world and then surrender to the result. This surrendering to the outcome is typically called giving up the "lust for result".

To succeed in magick, we have to be able to trust that it's working. We have to give up controlling how it's going to work as well. We don't have the ability to know every detail of everything that has to happen for our result to be realised.

Magick often works left of field. Things will line up in unexpected ways. Sometimes the magick works before a spell has even been cast.

Often the things we aren't so attached to are easier to manifest than things that are really important to us. It seems that strong emotional attachment to the result blocks the magick in some way. Perhaps it simply stifles the energy or prevents us from taking the right action towards allowing the results to flow into the manifest world. This receptive side of magick is often neglected and overlooked. It's not as exciting as the spell or ceremonial operation.

From a magickal point of view there are three worlds. The mental plane, the astral and the physical. We have a desire or an idea that is inspired in the mental plane, we then use magick to craft a template of that desire in the astral realm. The magick then manifests in the physical realm once we let go and psychologically create space for it to manifest.

In the law of attraction community, they call the astral "the vortex". They're not wrong either, the astral is like a swirling vortex of energy that crafts impressions, thoughts, feelings and ideas into the physical reality.

Essentially, magick allows us to be co-creators with the gods, spirits and universal forces of creation and destruction. Magick can be used to help us in a number of ways. It can help us create better living conditions, better health and attract love into our lives. It's great for influencing situations and people.

A love spell can bring the right person into your life or a career spell can land you a great job. Magick can help you increase your finances and investments. It can help you market your business and attract new customers, however, it has its limits.

Many people think that magick works wonders in the same way it does in the movies and fairy tales. We're constantly inundated with a lot of marketing about law of attraction. These gurus tell the tale of how they went from rags to riches simply through their thoughts.

Whether it's law of attraction of traditional magick it's usually presented as a quick fix. It's so easy, all you have to do is say some words, throw some herbs into a fire and poof stuff happens. It's really easy for us to fall into the habit of believing that magick is a simple answer to all of life's problems.

Of course, miracles happen and there are stories about miraculous results from magick. More often than not, the results are pretty mundane and unexciting.

Not all magick works either. Some spells work a little but don't really come through with the kind of results we want. Often the reasons why our magick doesn't pan out is more to do with our strategy and approach than with the magick itself. Other times no matter how much thought we put into a "working", it just doesn't give results.

There are a few things you've got to think about when it comes to magick. First, your goal needs to be realistic. One of the first spells I ever tried was to win the lottery. Of course, it failed. The probability of winning a jackpot in the lottery is pretty slim. All magick can do is increase the probability. It may help you win a small division but the jackpot isn't a realistic goal.

I receive emails all of the time from people who want me to cast a spell for them to become wealthy and successful. Like one spell is going to do that!

One of the reasons why magick doesn't always work the way we want is because the result we're looking for just isn't in our sphere of availability. In other words, it's not available to us in the environment in which we currently reside. This can be our physical environment as well as our mental/emotional environment.

For example, a money spell may bring you some money, however, that money has to come from somewhere. That somewhere has to be available to you. If you have a business or a job where you can earn more money through your performance a money spell will most likely bring you more money via that channel.

If you have money owing to you then you may receive that money, however, if you have no job, no business, nothing owing to you and no way to bring in an income then your spell may only bring you $50 that you find lying on the road.

So yes, money can come through an inheritance, lottery wins and other people but if you're really wanting wealth then you're going to have to create an environment in which that wealth can manifest.

This is where the sphere of availability comes in. Your

sphere of availability contains the things that are ready to come into your life. Most things happen step by step. You'll find that larger dreams and goals often require smaller steps before they materialise.

What comes into your sphere of availability are the things that you believe you can achieve and are able to receive. Each time you achieve something, more of it can filter into your sphere. Every time you progress in life physically, mentally or emotionally your sphere of availability expands to allow more of the things you want.

As the sphere widens, all of the situations, people and events that once seemed impossible can start flowing into your life. This is why it's so important to focus on the things you have already. It's also a good reason to celebrate every small step along the way to your goal. These small "wins" are like bread crumbs that lead the way to your major goal.

There are many ways in which you can expand your sphere of availability to include more of what you want. This is where being strategic with your spell crafting comes in. It's better to do many smaller spells than to rely on a big spell.

As an example, to become wealthy, you have to become a wealthy person in your mindset so that you will behave in a way that helps you accumulate wealth. You'll learn about investing, managing money and learning as much as you can about how to build wealth on a mundane level first. Then you use the magick to help you along the way.

Magick needs physical channels in order to manifest and that often requires us to set those up in non-magical ways. We have to take action in the mundane world and that is often something we don't want to do. Unfortunately, this is the major reason why our magick doesn't seem to work. The secret is to do the magick along the way for each next step rather than doing a magical spell and expecting a $20 million result. While some people do win the jackpot, most don't.

Unrealistic expectations about magick is called "magical thinking". You want to transform your approach from magical thinking to thinking magickally. When you're thinking magickally, you're thinking strategically. You'll be working your spells in alignment with each goal that you have. It's much like building a house. You'll have a plan first and then you'll build step by step until the house is completed. Big magickal goals are no different.

While you do need to plan, you don't need to know all of the details about how the magick is going to work. We leave the how to the magick. Through spell casting, we enchant for what we want and then leave the how to the universal forces to figure out.

Often, it's not the wealth or the money we really want, it's more the feelings of safety, security and freedom that come with wealth that we are wanting. There may be other ways to achieve these without focusing on having to make a lot of money.

A spiritual practice and shadow work can often take care of the real desires that we have. The fear of poverty and scarcity can often be alleviated through inner work.

When it comes to love magick it's no different. It's better for us to understand why we want a relationship in the first place. Is it out of need to feel loved or is it because we feel lonely? If we can learn to love ourselves first then we aren't so needy. If we can let go of the need then the magick can work to bring someone to us who may be better for us. It may even cause us to not even want to do a love spell after all.

Sometimes magick isn't the answer to our problems. A lot of people look to magick to help them feel better emotionally. I see so much of this going on in Facebook groups where people are asking for spells to help them cure anxiety or depression. Unfortunately, magick doesn't do a very good job at permanently changing emotional states. It can help with passing states, like sadness from a loss that has a natural process of healing. In some cases, magick can help soothe the path toward letting go.

The inner work and shadow work are really the only ways that help us alleviate unwanted emotional states like fear, anxiety and anger. Of course, if you struggle with any mental health condition it's always best to seek professional mental health assistance rather than rely on a spell to get you through.

The same goes for physical health conditions. Magick is more likely to help you find the best doctor or health practitioner who can help you. The magick can assist you to heal. Magick can influence the health practitioner's ability to make the right diagnosis and advise the best treatment. Use magick wisely, but don't go thinking it's the answer to every problem you encounter because sadly it's not.

When it comes to mental/emotional states there are some instances where magick can help you temporarily. If you're wanting to do a spell to help yourself feel more confident in a situation, you may be able to raise your level of confidence a little bit by doing a spell in the short term. However, in the long term if you're really wanting to raise your confidence then you'll need to do work decreasing self-doubt.

Our emotions are very helpful to us. If they weren't we

wouldn't have them. Although we don't want to be ruled by them, they are a guidance system, they tell us when something isn't right within ourselves. We can then use our discernment, intuition and rational thought to decide if action needs to be taken or not.

Spell Casting Ingredients and Correspondences

Pick up a book on spells and you'll find a list of ingredients in much the same way as you would a cooking recipe. There are herbs, stones, oils and candles. You'll probably see a chant or spell with instructions on what to do and when to do it.

All matter is 99% vibration. In magick we try to match our vibration to the frequency of our desire. When it comes to spell crafting, we work with items that energetically correspond to our desire. This works on the principle of like attracting like. Every colour, herb and gemstone has an energy or vibration that can magickally correspond to various desires or situations that we want to manifest.

This idea stems from the hermetic principle of correspondence which is where we get the phrase "As Above, So Below". For example, the colour pink corresponds to feelings of love and so we may burn a pink candle to attract love or friendship into our lives. Herbs such as cinnamon, basil or bay leaves correspond to money and so we may use them to attract money to us.

This is what differentiates magick from modern law of attraction. We use seemingly unrelated substances and tools to assist us in our manifestations. Vision boards are used in a similar way in law of attraction styles of spell crafting. This is a modern version of ancient cave painting where a successful hunt would be painted on a cave wall to link the desire for success to the action of hunting.

With a vision board you would cut out photographs and words that directly correspond to whatever it is you're wanting to manifest, for example, if you want a particular car then you would paste a photo of that car on your vision board. To add more magick to a vision board you could sprinkle it with herbs, recite an incantation over it and even place crystals upon it.

The Power of Words

Apart from using herbs or candles in our magick, we also use words. A spell really is a spoken request. The word "spell" means to speak something.

Words vibrate and when we state our request and feel into the desire as if it has already happened, our words vibrate at the same frequency as the desire.

This is why we must choose our words carefully. The universe often takes us literally so we have to be precise in our request. A lot of spells use rhythm to help us get into the vibrational flow. Other spells may just be one sentence or a few words that we repeat like a mantra.

The whole point is to be very clear about our desire and to state it in a way that makes us feel like it has already happened. It's not so much that you have to get emotionally excited, it's more that you feel it already being a reality.

Words influence us on a psychological level too. We can talk ourselves into feeling good or feeling bad. This is something to understand when it comes to choosing the right words for your spell.

The Power of Intention

Your desire should be as specific as you can make it. It could be along the lines of a new relationship, a new car, a better job, solving a particular problem or finding your life purpose.

Once you know the desire you can then become more exact in what you require, for example, you may want a particular type of job where you are doing specific tasks that you like and maybe even living in a location that you want to live in.

Often the magick won't bring you the exact results but it will bring you something similar. We think we know how something is going to work but magick often brings results in ways that we could never imagine. That's why we leave the how up the magick.

If you're struggling to be specific in your intention then you can easily break down what it is that you're really wanting. It's as simple as writing down what you don't want. Once you know what you don't want it's easier to know what you do want as an alternative.

This sounds easy enough but I want to mention that it is quite common for people to not to know what they really want. We've gone through our whole lives being told what we should want and what we shouldn't want that sometimes we just don't know.

We often knew what we wanted as children but so often these dreams and ambitions are stifled and discouraged. Many of us were even punished for expressing what we wanted. This can make knowing what we want very difficult.

Sometimes it's just been buried so deep within ourselves that we can't access it. There might be shame and guilt associated with what we want. These emotions can cause us to resist our true desire.

I've often been asked whether it's acceptable to do magick for personal gain. The answer is - of course it's acceptable. You are allowed to do magick for personal gain unless you are one of the characters of the original TV series "Charmed". You can do magick for pretty much anything that you want provided you're not overstepping your personal ethics. Creating is creating. There is no need to become hung up on being torn between spiritual and materiel goals. When we're on this planet we need both.

Sometimes, the material goals are needed to support a deeper purpose. Feel free to use your magickal ability to attract what you need on all levels. Be brave and dare to want. Dare to explore what you want.

Magick has the potential to help us tap into who we really are if we give it a chance. Sometimes we think a certain situation or person will make us happy when that's not the case at all. Magick works better when we align our desires to our higher spiritual will and our life path.

I knew someone who was doing magick to find a house to buy. She had the perfect idea of the perfect home. The magick came through for her but the home wasn't for sale, it was a rental. Perhaps her highest desire or will wasn't to own the home but simply to live in such a place.

Magick will often bring the results that stem from our subconscious beliefs rather than our conscious intentions, so it pays to "Know Thyself".

Spell Caster Checklist

The more you know yourself the easier it will be to plan you magick so that you're more likely to get the results that help you align with your life purpose.

Your aim is the first thing you need to discover. What are you wanting to get from your magick?

Let's look at some of the techniques you can use to find out what it is that you want. I use this technique in my book *Tapping into Abundance: Using EFT Tapping and Law of Attraction to Change Your Mindset and Turn Your Life Around.*

List what you don't want and then list what you would like instead next to each item.

Visualise your desire or perfect situation. Watch yourself living your desire. Spend about 5 minutes doing this. This is your opportunity to live your desire on the mental level so really go for it.

Act out who you are in this desired situation. You might want to lock yourself away from other people to do this or they might think you're a little crazy. Acting out is great if you aren't a visual person. You're creating on the astral level.

Record yourself telling a story about your perfect day. Make sure you mention who is there, where you are and what is around you. Be specific about what you want and break it down.

How do you expect to feel once you have that? It's important to know what you're going to feel once you have what it is that you want.

Are you expecting to feel fulfilled? Are you expecting to feel relief? What are you wanting to feel? The reason why we do magick in the first place is because we're trying to change the way we feel. We think that having a romantic relationship or more money is going to make us feel a certain way. It's actually the feeling we're after.

The feeling is important because this is what you need to focus on when you're doing the spell. Doing this first part may also cause you to realise that what you thought you wanted isn't necessary for you to feel the way you want to feel. You may even realise that there may be other options.

You also need to be realistic about the chances of your

spell actually being successful. Let's revisit winning the lotto. You may decide to try a spell the win $50 million. You've got thousands and thousands and thousands of other people also putting it out there to win that $50 million. You don't know how many other people might be doing law of attraction or spells to also try and win that $50 million so you've got a lot of competition there.

It would be better to ask yourself why you want $50 million anyway? Is it to get a sense of security? Is it so you can buy the things you want to buy? Maybe there are other ways that you can have what you want. Perhaps you'd be better off starting a business or learning how to invest. Then use magick to help you grow your business and increase the value of your investments.

Successful magick is often done in steps and stages. It's a lot like goal setting. You set the major goal first and work backwards. Do the same with magick. Do a grand spell for the big result and then work backwards until you work out the very next step you need to take to move you forward. Then do a spell for that if you need to.

As each spell completes and gives you results you can then move on to the next step and the next spell. It sounds like a lot of work and it is. This is real magick.

Often people come to spell casters either because they've tried everything else and it's a last resort or they're too lazy to do what needs to be done in the "real" world. If it's just a short-term goal then a one-off spell may be all you need. A lot of the time magick can be very simple.

Once you've completed your spell, let go of the lust for the result and follow the crumbs as the magick leads you to take action in the real world.

Sometimes there may be obstacles in the way of your

desire. If you know what those obstacles are you can do magick to remove them. This is where road opener spells can work wonders. Sometimes a road opener is all you need.

It's also important to have a look at some of your inner obstacles to achieving your goals. Limiting beliefs like "I'm not good enough" or "I don't deserve" can block success. You can energetically cancel your spell if you feel undeserving or inadequate in any way. The biggest danger of psychological blocks is that they can stop you from taking the action that is required for the spell to complete.

Often, you'll be offered an idea or result but you won't act on it. This is why magick usually fails. It's not the magick it's the lack of follow through. Now this doesn't mean that you have to act on everything magick brings to you. Sometimes the results will not be suitable. In that case adjust your spell and cast again.

Spell Crafting

When it comes to the actual spell itself then you need to think about what supplies you're going to need. If you're going to do candle magick, you'll need a candle. If you're going to work with colour then you'll need to understand colour correspondences. Here is a list of colours and their magickal correspondences:

Black – Banishing and curse removal
White – Healing, cleansing and purifying
Red – Passion, courage, confidence
Orange – Success, attainment, well being
Yellow – Communication, Mental Clarity, Study
Green – Money, growth, fertility
Blue – Peace, healing, soothing
Purple – Psychism, intuition, wealth

Brown – Home, garden, stability
Pink – Love, relationships, compassion

If you're doing love magick you can use a pink candle. A green candle is traditionally chosen for money spells and blue for healing.

When you write your spell make sure it flows well. Many people like to use rhyme. The rhythm of poetry does help create a connection energetically with your desire. You can even break your desire up into key words and chant them like a mantra.

While you're chanting your spell, visualise your desire and emotionally experience it as if it has already happened. Trust that the deities and spirits that you are working with will come through for you.

As witches, we work with the lunar phases to help the magick along. Do you want something to grow and build? Then do the spell during a waxing moon. Are you trying to release or bring something to an end, then do the spell during a waning moon?

If you want a lot of power behind your spell then do it as close to the full moon as possible. Astrologically, the full moon is a time of release so doing spell work at this time can accelerate the results.

How are you going to raise the energy? Are you going to chant your spell multiple times? It's often useful to chant your spell three, seven or nine times. You can also dance to raise the energy as you chant.

Once the spell has been cast it's time to relax and get on with life. Act as if the spell has worked and follow your intuition, taking note of any opportunities or ideas that present themselves to you.

You may be inspired to go to a party or gathering where you'll meet your next great love, or a job opportunity may present itself to you. Follow the crumbs and be discerning. Remember you don't always have to accept the results.

Magick is not always easy and it can take time to achieve results. It's not like it is in the movies.

To help you plan your magick I have a free PDF available for download on my website called the **Spell Caster Checklist**. It will help you get specific about what you want and guide you toward successful spell planning.

https://tinyurl.com/spellcasterchecklist

You can find some simple spells to perform by going to my YouTube channel and accessing the Spells and Magick playlist: https://www.youtube.com/c/MysticalWitchSchool

The Lunar Rites

Chapter Seven

I remember the first time I did a lunar rite by myself. I was chanting the names of the goddess while moving around in a circle raising energy and it was one of the most exhilarating feelings that I ever had. I could really feel that energy of the moon coming down into me. It was powerful.

When I was in my first coven, we only did full moon rites. We never celebrated the new moon. The three days leading up to the new moon were the witch's holiday and a time for introspection. There was no spell casting during these three days of the dark moon. We were encouraged to use this time for divination and inner work.

The moon is associated with the Goddess as it ties in with the monthly menstrual cycle. As Wiccans, we honour the moon's twenty-nine-day cycle beginning with the new moon. The new moon is that thin sliver of a crescent that you see in the sky after a three-day period of hardly seeing the moon at all. The moon then spends two weeks waxing, getting larger and larger each day until she's at the height of her power at the full moon. She then begins to wane for another two weeks until the return of the next new moon and the cycle begins again.

Witches work with the moon ritually and magickally. We blend our magick with her cycle of growth and decay.

We utilise these cycles in our magick to know when to cast spells for growth and when to banish and release what we no longer want.

We also honour the Goddess in her aspects of maiden, mother and crone during the lunar cycle. The new moon corresponds to the maiden, the mother is symbolised by the full moon and the waning and dark moons are associated with the crone.

All three stages of growth, bloom and decay are honoured and celebrated in Wicca as they are the cycles of life and rebirth. These cycles remind us that life is full of ups and downs. We learn how to navigate these tides through our inner work and through the use of magick.

The Full Moon

The full moon has always been associated with witches throughout modern history. There are paintings and stories about witches dancing naked under the full moon throughout the centuries. When witchcraft made its comeback in the 1960s it was common for covens to dance naked under the moon, however, that doesn't seem to be as popular these days.

The full moon has a very strong pull on the earth. We know that it affects the tides, plants and water in the soil. The moon has a very close connection with water, that's why you can often feel quite emotional as the moon nears full in her cycle.

This emotional pull can certainly help us in our magick. When we have more emotional energy working within us, we also have more power. As the moon waxes or grows in strength we are able to harness more of her energy for spell work.

Astrologers usually associate the full moon with release. This is true and as witches we use this time of

release to send out our most powerful ma'
moon also lights up in the sky at night, refl'
of the sun. She has a reflective energy so wh...
she is also giving us some of the strong solar li.
reflective nature of the moon reminds us how the ᴄ
verse gives back what we put out.

At this time the moon is in opposition to the sun as well so you'll also feel opposing energies between the astrological signs and houses that the sun and moon are in. You can use these energies in your magick. For example, if the sun is in Virgo and the moon in Pisces you can work to combine the analytical and logical aspects of Virgo with the dreamy and illusory aspects of Pisces.

To celebrate the full moon, you really only need yourself and the moon. Stand outside under the moonlight and feel the light shining upon you. Notice the shades of grey around you and the luminescent shimmering light on your skin. Breathe in the light and feel the connection to your psychic intuitive self. You can say:

Lady of the Full Moon,
Known by many names,
Luna, Selene, Mene,
Bless me with your light.

The Benefits of Drawing Down the Moon

In Wicca, we do a ceremony called "Drawing Down the Moon". In a traditional Wiccan coven, the high priest draws down the energy of the moon into the high priestess. There's also a ritual called drawing down the Sun where the high priestess will draw the energy of the sun into to the high priest.

As solitaries we draw these into ourselves. What we're doing is connecting with that magnetic energy of the on to make ourselves more magnetic to what we want. e do the same with the sun to draw in the solar energies.

Drawing down the lunar energy also connects us to the lunar deities. Through the light of the moon, we can draw the essence of the deities into ourselves. We can then use that energy for spell work, divination and connecting to the feminine energy.

Many witches like to collect moon water to use later in spell work, rituals and scrying. To do this consecrate and cleanse a bowl of water and leave it out under the full moon light from dusk to dawn. Be careful to remove it before the sun rises.

Use this water to enhance your psychic abilities, scrying and to anoint candles and talismans.

The New Moon

Technically, the new moon is that first thin crescent you see in the sky at the beginning of the lunar cycle. Astrologically, it is usually a couple of days before that. The phase before the new moon is the dark moon phase. This is usually a three-day period before you see the first sliver of silver in the sky.

The new moon marks the time for growth and new beginnings. It's the perfect time for planting new seeds literally or metaphorically. This is the time to do spell work for growth, beginnings and replacing the old with the new.

Sometimes your spells will need the energy of the full moon and other times you'll want a slow build. Many spells are better suited to a slower building or scaffolding especially so if you're creating something like a business, study program or even a relationship.

The new moon is a very important time for spell craft, possibly more so than the full moon. This is because it's during the waxing phase that the growth happens. I do most of my magic during this part of the lunar cycle rather than hitting it with a full moon blast.

Astrologically, the new moon will always be in the same sign as the sun. So that means if you are doing your spell work and the sun is in Virgo the new moon will be in Virgo as well. This will lend very strong practical Virgoan energy to your spell.

The moon moves through the zodiac signs approximately every two days. You can always look up a moon chart to see when the moon will be in a sign that is favourable to the kind of magical work you're wanting to do.

I tend to do magic on the fly and so I don't worry too much about what zodiac sign the moon is in. If I need to do magic then I do it.

To celebrate the new moon, light a candle and say the following:

Lady of the New Moon,
Known by many names throughout the world,
Hekate, Diana, Artemis,
Bless me as I celebrate the cycle of endings and beginnings.

The Dark Moon

The dark moon is a term that witches use to denote the time when you can't see the moon at all in the sky because it is in such a position that it isn't reflecting the sun. This happens a couple of days before the new moon.

During this time witches will utilise the darkness for introspection and divination. When I was in my first coven, we were told to never do magick three days before the new moon as the spells may not work or could backfire.

I don't believe that this is true. It's more about the energy declining which can affect the energy behind the spell.

Moon Void of Course

In astrology, the moon is said to be void of course when it's left one zodiac sign but hasn't fully transitioned into the next.

Astrologically the moon influences our emotions so all of her aspects and cycles have the potential to affect us emotionally. The theory is that when this happens, we are left in an emotional limbo.

Our goal as magick workers isn't to be like the jellyfish totally governed by the planets. Magick allows us to raise ourselves so that we aren't as susceptible to the planetary influences. Although we work with the lunar cycles, there is more to magick than the moon.

Our ability to use other influences through correspondences and our intention and focus hold power as well so don't let the moon void of course stop you from doing a spell if delaying your spell work causes you more problems.

Many people will say that you shouldn't do magick during a void of course moon because the moon energetically doesn't have much influence. I haven't found this to be true in magick. Maybe in astrology it has a subtle influence but not in magick.

I was never taught to consider the void of course moon in my magical training with my high priest and high priestess. It's not something that is considered in ceremonial magick or hermetic magick either.

While astrology is important it is only an influence. It doesn't totally determine who we are and what we can or can't do. As magick workers we have the ability to lessen astrological influences through becoming more self-aware and stronger in our aim.

If we can fully create our desire in the astral then planetary influences can help but they aren't necessary for success.

The Sabbats

Chapter Eight

Like all religions, Wicca has its holy days and celebrations. We call them Sabbats and they occur throughout the year. Our sabbats are celebrations of the changing seasons and collectively they make up the Wiccan Wheel of the year.

Whereas the lunar rites are focused more upon the divine feminine, the sabbats are solar in nature and focus on the God of the witches as well as the Goddess. These sabbats are rites of celebration and reverence connecting us to the earth, the stars and the sun.

We have eight sabbats which are spaced approximately six weeks apart. They include the solstices, equinoxes and seasonal observances in-between. During these cycles we know when it's time to plant new seeds both literally and figurately. We know when to harvest what we've planted and when it is time to rest, rejuvenate and consolidate. These activities stem from the original pagans who lived in agricultural communities.

The sabbats originated in various European cultures and we have modernised them to suit our current times. Celebrating the sabbats helps us to connect to the cycles of the earth and to our own cycles. They help us connect to the principle of polarity, of scarcity, plenty, dark and light. The sabbats help us to understand that there's a time to create and there's a time to destroy and that these opposing aspects are necessary for the continuation of life on Earth. There is no judgement. Day is no better than night. Light is not always good and darkness is not evil.

Our ancestors celebrated these times to magickally encourage the fertility of the earth and to enjoy the fruits of their labours. Sabbats are times for rejoicing and offering gratitude and appreciation for an abundant harvest.

The sabbats teach us about surrendering to the flow of creation and life. We can learn to let go of the incessant need to control everything in our lives. The seasons are very much out of our control. We have to learn to live with nature and not try to constantly dominate her.

Nature teaches us that we can't always get what we want. She teaches us how to take responsibility for our wellbeing. Through her we learn about the harsh reality of existence. We learn that we are all equal under nature, however, not every animal has the same opportunities as other animals. Some animals are born in abundant locations full of food and water, while other animals are born in areas ravaged by drought and scarcity. Each animal has to make the best of their circumstances. The successful animals learn how to overcome their limitations.

The dark and light aspects of nature teach us about life. We learn how important it is to take responsibility for our own lives. Witches don't see ourselves as victims, we take initiative and create what we want. Even though it may be difficult at times, we don't give our power away by blaming others for our circumstances.

We divide our sabbats into two categories, the greater sabbats and lesser sabbats. The greater sabbats are celebrations of the changing of the seasons, while the lesser sabbats mark the middle of the season. We also call the greater sabbats the cross-quarter days as they mark the transition from autumn to winter, winter to spring, spring to summer and summer to autumn.

The lesser sabbats are the Winter and Summer Solstices and Autumn and Spring Equinoxes. These mark the position of the Sun in relation to the Earth's equator. Although we divide them into greater and lesser sabbats, they are equal in importance.

The greater sabbats are believed to fall on days of greater power. They were originally celebrated on a full moon where both the solar and lunar energies are at their most powerful. The greater sabbats were celebrated over two days. They started in the evening on the first day and continued throughout the whole of the next day.

In modern times we can celebrate the sabbats on three levels. The first is through meditation on the seasonal changes we are witnessing around us. The second level is psychological, where we can take time out to observe how we feel about various seasons and how they affect us energetically. This helps us learn more about ourselves. The sabbats can mirror our cycles of ups and downs, peaks and troughs.

The third and most important level is spiritual. We can learn how our spiritual evolution is also cyclical. We have times of amazing spiritual epiphanies and other times we plateau out. Sometimes, we find ourselves in spiritual valleys when we experience those dark nights of the soul. Tuning into the cycles of the year helps us process the mental and emotional experiences so that they become opportunities for self-knowledge.

Let's take a look at the eight sabbats.

Samhain

As humans, we tend to think in concrete ways. We believe in beginnings and endings, yet when we look at nature there is only transformation.

Samhain marks the beginning of the Wiccan yearly cycle. It's not a beginning though, it's more of recognition of our cyclical existence. With every ending there is a beginning and Samhain represents both endings and beginnings.

As witches, we acknowledge that beginnings and endings aren't final, they are simply a change from one state into another. Samhain is a time of transformation honouring the life cycle of death and decay.

Samhain possibly means summers end. It comes after autumn and was the Celtic new year. It was celebrated traditionally during the full moon. The Christianised name is All Hallows Eve or Halloween.

In modern Wicca, Samhain is celebrated in the northern hemisphere on October the 31st and November 1st, which falls within the constellation of Scorpio. In the southern hemisphere Samhain is celebrated on April 30th and May the 1st and falls within the sign of Taurus.

The astrological signs influence the energy of the sabbats and it's quite likely that the original pagans incorporated astrology into their seasonal cycles. Scorpio is associated with transformation and death whereas Taurus is connected more with fertility and growth. As I live in Australia, I do find the Samhain energy here quite bright and lively even in the southern regions that experience the four seasons.

According to the Celts, the new year begins in the darkness of Samhain. It is in the darkness of the soil that a seed begins to sprout. The infant gestates in the darkness of the womb. The dark can be a nurturing place, a safe place. The dark can provide a comforting place to begin the delicate transition from No Thing into a Some Thing.

This is what we mean when we say darkness in Wicca. The dark isn't a place of evil and harmfulness. It's simply an absence of light. The darkness is the primal state. The light comes from the dark. No one has invented a dark switch yet. We turn on the light, or shine a light into the darkness to see more clearly.

From a hermetic perspective consciousness gives birth to itself out of the darkness through the spark of inspiration. This spark penetrates a container in which the inspiration can develop into a form. The spark of inspiration is masculine energy and the container is the feminine. Consciousness itself is androgynous.

Coming back down to planet earth where we rely on her produce for survival, Samhain marks the last harvest. Traditionally, at Samhain, it was time to reap and store as much as possible for the long cold winter ahead.

In traditional Wicca, Samhain is also the time when the veil between the worlds of the living and the dead is the thinnest. This is a time when many witches will communicate with loved ones who have passed over.

The place where the dead reside is called the Summerland. This concept of the Summerland seems to have its roots in Swedenborg and Theosophy. To many Wiccans the Summerland isn't a place but rather a state in which the consciousness resides until the next incarnation.

Most Wiccans believe in reincarnation. The idea that life continues in many forms is common in most religions, especially those of pagan origin. We understand that energy never dies, it just changes form. We notice that nothing truly disappears, it just morphs into something else. It seems to make sense that spirit does the same.

Wiccans also believe in karma. The concept of karma differs depending on the school of origin though. In western culture, our understanding of karma stems from theosophy and doesn't resemble the eastern concept. Due to our Judaeo-Christian background, westerners tend to see karma as a system of reward and punishment.

From an eastern perspective Karma is more about what we focus upon in life and how that reflects back at us in following lives. We reap the results of our projections.

The idea of karma being a reward and punishment system never made sense. Who were the karmic police? Who is the judge? It makes more sense to me that what we project out and are preoccupied with creates the karmic results.

To me this sounds very much like magick. What you focus on is what you get. A life spent focusing on compassion, love and personal growth is more likely to improve your future lives. This means that when you come back to Earth, you're more likely to have a favourable rebirth.

If you are living a life where there's a propensity towards destruction and harmfulness whether it's towards yourself or towards others then this will negatively affect your future life and this one too!

So, it's not about reward and punishment because there is no one to reward or punish in the pagan philosophy. It's simply what you project reflects back to you which is nothing like the karma that we're told from the Theosophical tradition.

Samhain is a time to reflect on death and the meaning of life. You may have already had the experience of being with a person or animal when they have passed. It is indeed an honour to be present at a passing. It's an important reminder that nothing lasts forever in its current state. Life is full of flux. We are reminded that we too will die. When we realise this, we can then ask ourselves these important questions: What am I doing with my life? How do I make my life meaningful?

From a Wiccan point of view Samhain is as much about remembering and honouring our ancestors as it is about honouring the changing season. You may want to do meditations or offerings to your own ancestors at this time.

Remembrance Rite by the Sea

This rite is a beautiful rite to perform by the sea, however, if that's not possible then find a natural water source like a lake, creek or river. You can perform this rite in memory of a person or animal who has passed over.

Choose a flower for each person who has passed over whom you want to honour during this rite. As you sit by the water reflect on the life of this person. Feel the joy as you remember them, you may feel their presence as you do this. Speak to them, telling them how you love them and wish them well on their new journey. When you feel the time is right, take the flowers and cast them into the ocean.

On a psychological level, Samhain can be a time to reflect on what needs to be released from your life in order for you to continue to grow. It can be a time of letting go of habits and unhelpful belief systems. You can honour your past and give gratitude for how it has helped you get where you are. Even if you're not where you want to be or you feel regret about the past, your past actions have still brought you here into the present. It's in the present moment that you can proceed with a fresh slate. You no longer need to carry the burdens from the past, you can let them go at this time.

Spiritually, it's a time to reflect on your practice. Where does it need changing? Have you been living your practice as much as you want to? How can you incorporate your practice into your daily routine in the next year to bring more meaning into your life?

Give yourself the space during this time to enjoy the safety of the darkness and the new possibilities it can bring you.

Yule

Yule is derived from the ancient Germanic calendar. It's a winter festival celebrating the birth of the Sun God. In the Celtic lands there is a competitive dual between the Oak and Holly Kings. This is a Wiccan rite that focuses more on the God than the Goddess.

Astrologically, it is the winter solstice, the shortest day of the year. A time when the night is long, cold and dark. At this time the Sun God is born of the Mother Goddess. It's a common theme found in many cultures around the world. During this time the sun is at his weakest but as of the next day he starts to gradually grow in strength. That's why it is celebrated as his birth.

In the northern hemisphere, Yule can fall anywhere from 19th to the 23rd of December. Whereas in the southern hemisphere it falls anywhere between the 19th to the 23rd of June.

Yule is that time of year when there is the least amount of sun light. The Samhain theme of dwelling safely in the dark continues throughout this time. In places that experience long winters with chilling temperatures this time of year is a big deal. In the past, people had to plan ahead for winter because food was scarce during this time. In many places it's not even possible to go outside at certain times due to snow levels.

These extremes of nature remind us of our vulnerability. This means that Yule can be a time where we can learn how to warm ourselves when we are feeling most raw and vulnerable. Vulnerability is seen as a weakness and it's something few of us want to admit we experience. Yet, all of us are vulnerable to the whims of Nature.

On a psychological level, realising where we are vulnerable physically, emotionally and mentally can help us learn to ask for help and take ownership of our needs. Owning our vulnerability makes us more responsible for ourselves and for others. Once we understand our own vulnerabilities it makes it easier to have empathy for other people.

Becoming aware of our vulnerabilities can help us know what we may need to do to protect and nurture ourselves. Realising that every human being on this planet has vulnerabilities connects us as humans to each other.

In the northern hemisphere, Capricorn rules over Yule whereas in the southern hemisphere it is in the season of Cancer. Capricorn can bring a very stabilising aspect to Yule whereas Cancer is more nurturing.

Traditionally, bonfires were lit to celebrate the coming of the light. You'll find that bonfires feature in most of the sabbats that's why they are also referred to as fire festivals.

Yule is a wonderful time of year where I live. The sun is warm and I love going down to the beach in the middle of the day. I sit on my rock and meditate while enjoying the clear calm water. That doesn't sound much like a traditional yule, yet it's a typical Yuletide where I live.

It's important to take notice of what winter looks and feels like where you live. If you have snow that's wonderful if not that's good too.

As this is the darkest time of the year it's a good time to plant the seeds of peace, calm and balance for the coming year. Plan what you want to bring into your life this coming year. Ask yourself, how and where are you going to plant new seeds in your life?

Magickally, it's a good time to do prosperity spells. Money is the energy of life in our modern world. It's very difficult to live without it. Money is the seed, the grain, the shelter and the comfort these days so don't overlook its importance in your life.

Take advantage of the cold weather and make yourself a warm money bath with the help of the Celtic God Cernunnos:

Cernunnos Prosperity Bath

Ingredients:

Bay Leaves
Cinnamon Stick
Citrine Crystal

Put the bay leaves and cinnamon stick in some boiling water. Allow the brew to cool and then add the citrine crystal. Stand for 3 hours as the herbs infuse into the water. After 3 hours, strain the mix and discard the herbs. You can bury them in the south east corner of your property or place in a pot plant. You can place the citrine in the south east corner of your home or carry it with you.

Run yourself a bath and pour in the herbal infusion. As you take the bath imagine yourself having everything you need for a healthy and happy life. See yourself doing what you want to be doing and having what you want and need to have. As you do this say:

Lord of the Wildwood,
Lord of abundant provision,
Show me the path to financial prosperity,
As I dwell in energies of cinnamon, bay and citrine,
Open the forest doors of my mind to wealth.

If you don't have a bathtub then mix the herbal infusion with some warm water and pour it over yourself as you take a shower. Alternatively, place the mixture into a basin of water and enjoy a birdbath, by spreading the water along your arms, face and neck.

Imbolc

In the northern hemisphere Imbolc falls on the 1st and 2nd of February, whereas in the southern hemisphere it occurs on the 1st and 2nd of August.

In the Christian calendar it's known as Candlemas and is celebrated in both the Liberal and Roman Catholic Churches.

The astrological influences are Aquarius in the northern hemisphere and Leo in the southern hemisphere. Aquarius lends its influence of inspiration to the sabbat and Leo adds the fiery light of inspired passion.

At Imbolc we celebrate new growth. We see the first signs of spring as the ice begins to melt and new growth begins to pop its head out of the still soil. It's the celebration of the end of winter and falls halfway between the winter solstice and the spring equinox. The word Imbolc, most likely means ewes milk and signals the stirrings of spring.

If you live in a region of the world where you experience long dark cold winters then you can probably relate to the joy you feel when you start to see the first buds of grass coming up through the snow. For people living closer to the equator, it's generally not such a big deal but we can still celebrate the meaning on a more energetic level.

At this time of year, it starts becoming more noticeable that the sun's light is gaining more strength and you'll begin to notice that the Sun is starting to rise further towards the centre of the sky. That's why Imbolc is also called the feast of lights. The sky is becoming brighter once more.

In the northern hemisphere this day is also Groundhog Day and this has its roots in Celtic myth as well. The Cailleach, or crone in Scottish mythology ventures out to gather firewood for the remaining winter during this time. It is said that if it is a sunny day she is put into a foul mood.

In Celtic mythology the Cailleach is a dark aspect of the goddess and is the bringer of death and often brings in storms and westerly winds during this time. When she is in this foul mood, she draws more of the winter cold around her thus causing extra cold weeks.

Depending on where you live in the world there's definite changes going on in the weather. The Cailleach is the one who brings the right weather to stir the change of seasons. She is she transforming crone energy after all.

Spend some time observing what nature is doing right now around you. Where you live informs how you go about your life. How is it affecting you physically, emotionally and spiritually?

On a psychological level you may want to think about what new energy you want to bring into your life right now and for the coming year.

Spend some time with your journal dwelling on what inspires you. What drives you to practice your spiritual craft? What inspires you to create at all? Where does your inspiration lie?

What changes are you making right now in your life? What changes do you want to make and how are you going to make them?

It's traditional to celebrate Imolc by lighting a candle on Imbolc eve and setting it in a window sill. Of course, if this isn't safe to do so then it's not necessary. The candle symbolises light and inspiration.

Imbolc is also associated with the Celtic Goddess Brigid. She is a goddess of healing, inspiration and creativity. She is a patron goddess of blacksmiths and artists. Working with her during this time can help you find the inspiration to start something new as the weather warms and motivation begins to wax.

Ask Brigid to give you visions of how you can manifest new projects through fire scrying. If you have a fireplace you can gaze into the flames as you ask Brigid to guide your sight. Otherwise, light a candle and ask the Goddess Brigid to reveal to you what inspires you the most and how you can bring that light of inspiration into your world right now.

Goddess Brigid of the forge,
Guide my sight as I gaze upon the flames,
Show me where my true path leads,
Light my way, light my way.

Ostara

Both the spring and autumn equinoxes symbolize a seasonal transition point where you're moving from the cooler months into the warmer months or the warmer months into the cooler months. There is also a psychic transition that accompanies that seasonal change so they have energetic importance, however, they're a relatively recent addition to the northern European celebrations.

The spring equinox is otherwise known as Ostara and is named after the German dawn goddess. This goddess doesn't actually seem to exist much in the Germanic mythology so there's a debate about whether Ostara is actually a deity.

Even though there's a lack of evidence to suggest there was such a goddess it doesn't necessarily mean there wasn't. Nonetheless she now exists in the Wiccan festivities during this time.

You'll also find Ostara referred to as Eostre which is Old English for Ostrow and it means the bringer of light. There are very strong associations with the Roman goddess Venus as well via this imagery.

In the southern hemisphere Ostara occurs from the 19th to 21st of September and in the northern hemisphere it can occur anywhere between the 19th to 21st of March.

In the southern hemisphere the Sun is entering the zodiac sign of Libra which is a sign of balance and harmony associated with the planet Venus. In the northern hemisphere the sun is moving into Aries which has a more passionate masculine energy.

During the spring equinox we focus on the implementation of the ideas we began to forge during Imbolc. We focus more energy to initiate new projects and birth them into the world. It's common for covens to do initiations at this time.

Magickally, it's time to do spell work to create new beginnings, make magickal bags, charms and talismans. Many witches recharge their tools at this time and also clean their space more thoroughly.

Whether it's magical bags to help you grow your money in the coming year or a candle spell to attract new love into your life, spring is a great season for enchantments.

Spring is a continuation of the energy of Imbolc so many of the introspective and reflective activities will still have relevance to you now. Revisit the questions you asked yourself during Imbolc and see if you have more to add to them. How have they changed? What may be new?

Ritual Spring Clean to Remove Unwanted Energy from Your Home

Ingredients:

Clove buds
Eucalyptus leaves
Rosemary leaves

Boil some water and add the herbs to the water. Infuse the herbs in the water for 3 hours. After 3 hours, strain the mixture and discard the herbs. You can sprinkle them outside the front door if you wish.

Place the herbal water in a bucket with warm water and use it to mop the floors of your home. Mop from the back door to the front door. If you have carpets place the herbal water into a spray bottle and spray your home beginning from the back door to the front door.

This will clear any unwanted energy from your home.

Beltane

Beltane is named after the Celtic god Belenus which means our bright one or shining one. It's a celebration of sexuality, life and fertility. It was a time when ancient people would drive the cattle through the ashes of their

CRAFTING YOUR WICCAN PATH

sacred Beltane balefire to their summer pastures.

The balefire was used to symbolise fiery passion and couples who were married would jump the fire to ensure a fertile union.

In the northern hemisphere Beltane occurs April 30th to May the 1st and in the southern hemisphere it's October the 31st to the 1st November. The fertile energy of Taurus is present in the northern hemisphere at this time whereas the watery sexuality of Scorpio features in the southern hemisphere.

Traditionally, Beltane is the celebration and encouragement of reproduction, fertilisation of the soil and fattening the herd. It's a great time of year of attending your garden and focusing on nourishing the soul.

In traditional Wicca, the Goddess and God are married at Beltane. In Irish myth the Dagda is associated with Beltane as well as the May Queen. The May Queen doesn't have a name she's just known as the May Queen. The god aspect of course is Balanus.

The masculine and feminine energies unite at this time neutralising and reconciling opposites. It's through the reconciling of binaries that a new beginning can emerge. This dance of the Goddess and God is depicted during the Maypole dance where the pole signifies the phallus and the ribbons the vagina.

The Celts didn't demonise sexuality, it was simply a part of being alive and celebrating life. The Maypole dance is one of the remaining festivals that is very much about acceptance and reverence towards sexuality.

The Maypole dance symbolises the law of three in occultism where the one joins with two and they become three. It's a celebration of the ternary in western hermeticism. It's the reconciling of opposites to produce something that is workable and sustainable.

Life doesn't emerge from only one pole. Extremes of polarity don't produce life, in fact they will stall it and even destroy it. It's when two extremes or differences merge together that life continues. This third force is the magick. This third force is where we get to create evolution and growth.

Beltane is the time of year when we can ponder the deeper meanings of esoteric laws and see how they are reflected in our current world. There have always been extremes of ideologies, religions and politics. Humanity is largely third force blind meaning that we stick to one side of an idea and refuse to consider another point of view or concern. This way of thinking only causes divisiveness and destruction. It's the coming together of opposites that creates harmony.

Too much light is blinding and too much dark is also blinding. Too much heat is dangerous and unbearable so is too much cold. Reflect on the sweet spot in the middle.

Your magick at this time can be focused on fertility, growth, abundance and creation. Of course, love magick features highly for people at this time too.

I find that this season inspires me toward more creative pursuits. Often new passions or even old ones will become enlivened during this time. Some questions to ask yourself are: How can I bring more passion, joy and growth into my life? Where do I fall prey to extremes of thinking? How can I bring creative balance to opposing aspects of my life?

Beltane Love Spell

Ingredients:

Pink candle
Rose oil or rose petals

Anoint your candle with the rose oil making sure to start at the tip of the candle and rubbing the oil down the candle all the way to the bottom. If you're using rose petals, anoint the candle with olive oil and then roll the candle in the rose petals.

Light the candle and say:

Candle pink with scented rose bring my love to me,
Shine your light throughout the world and send my love my way,
The love within my heart burns bright,
Surrounding me with joy,
Before me, behind me, above and below me,
I see my love with me.

Litha

At Litha, we celebrate the summer solstice. The word solstice means sun standstill so in the case of Litha the sun appears to be standing still in the centre of the sky above us.

In the northern hemisphere the summer solstice is anywhere between the 19th to the 23rd of June and in the southern hemisphere anywhere between the 19th and the 23rd of December. The solstices and equinoxes don't always fall on the same date because they are determined by the rotation and tilt of the earth as it moves around the Sun.

The Zodiac sign of Cancer gives the summer solstice a nurturing energy in the northern hemisphere whereas, Capricorn gives the solstice a very grounded and productive energy in the southern hemisphere.

Litha is the opposite of Yule in its energy. Whereas Yule is the darkest time, Litha is the brightest time. The Sun is at the peak of his heat and power. It's the time to celebrate growth and high energy. Magickally you can give projects a boost of solar energy at this time.

The mother goddesses and vegetation gods are popular at this time due to their association with the fertile earth. The Goddess Cerridwen and her cauldron are honoured and celebrated alongside of the God in his Green Man aspect.

If there is a time for empowerment and success magick it's during this season. If you've got something that you've been working on or wanting to build, give it a big energetic blast now.

It's traditionally the time of hand fasting (Wiccan marriage), renewal and fertility celebrated around bonfires.

Litha reaches the peak of the energy of Beltane. It is from this point onwards that the year begins to wane and the harvest seasons begin. Personally, I feel that Litha is a time to simply celebrate life and the abundance that we have already. The questions to ask yourself are: What am I grateful for? How can I show my gratitude and appreciation for what I have right now?

Ring of Gratitude

Ingredients:

Daisies (to make a daisy ring)
Paper, pen and scissors
White Candle

Cut the paper into smaller pieces and on each piece write down what you are grateful for. Weave your daisies together in a ring and add your paper with your gratitude statements to the ring.

Light your candle and say the following while holding up your ring of gratitude:

At this time and place,
I call to the Goddess, mother of all,
Lady of the Moon and fertile earth, I give thanks for all you have bestowed upon me,
At this time and place,
I call to the God, Green Man of the fields,
Lord of the Sun, of forests and the hunt, I give thanks for all you have provided for me.

This ring of gratitude I offer,
This ring of appreciation I give,
Lord and Lady, please accept my gratitude,
Blessed BE!

Lughnasadh

Lughnasadh is named after the Celtic god Lugh who is most associated with light and fire. In the northern hemisphere it falls on the 1st and 2nd of August and in the southern hemisphere it is the 1st and 2nd of February.

In the northern hemisphere the zodiac influence is Leo and in the Southern hemisphere it is Aquarius. Leo adds the energy of passion during this time while Aquarius adds a more inspired energy.

Lughnasadh is the celebration of the first harvest, particularly of grains and cereals. These were the foods that people would be gathering and storing for the coming winter months. A good harvest was necessary for survival through the cold dark barren times of winter.

If you live in a city, you probably don't feel the urgency around food during this season as food is generally plentiful. It can be difficult to imagine what life would be like without an easy supply of food all year round.

These sabbats make us aware of how vulnerable we are. We are still reliant upon nature. Climate changes and cataclysmic weather can ruin crops and cause food shortages even in our own times. Nature is still in control.

Lughnasadh was the time of year when the Celts would conduct temporary hand fastings, marriages that would span a year and a day. At the end of that year the couple could decide to get married again for another year or they could part ways.

The deities most celebrated at Lughnasadh are the Morrigan, Brigid and Lugh. The god Lugh was worshiped in Ireland as a deity of the Sun. This connection with the Sun most likely explains his name (it means "shining one"), and it also may account for his attributes such as handsomeness, perpetual youth and tremendous energy and vitality.

In Irish mythology, Lugh dedicated this time to hold funeral games in honour of his foster-mother, Tailtiu, who died after clearing the land to make way for agriculture. Forests once covered the land and when people became farmers, the land was cleared and the forests began to vanish.

The name Lughnasadh incorporates the word "nasadh", meaning "binding promise". This stems from the myth where Lugh makes a promise to Tailtiu to hold funeral games in her honour. So, when the celts wanted to make an oath that could never be broken they would invoke the four elements.

As a harvest rite Lughnasadh is all so about celebrating what you've reaped. It's a time to express gratitude for what you've accomplished.

It's also a great time to do rituals for blessings and con-secrations. You may want to consecrate your tools again or do blessings and protection magick for your home, ve-hicle and work space.

On a psychological level, Lughnasadh is a time to reflect on what you have achieved over the last twelve months. Take notice of how you have grown and where in your life you have made changes. You are harvesting at this time so ponder what you are harvesting.

Spiritually, recall how your practice has contributed to your life. How has it enhanced your life? How has it given your life more meaning?

You may want to do a self-dedication rite to honour your commitment to your spiritual path. It's not an oath like the ancient celts made with the elements, think of it more like a statement of intent. In the dedication rite below you will be calling upon Lugh to assist you on your path.

Lughnasadh Self Dedication Rite

On this harvest day I call upon the God Lugh,
God of fire and light,
Pay witness to my intent to walk a path of light.
I call upon the element of Air,
Inspire my thoughts with love,
I call upon the element of Fire,
Protect me on my path.
I call upon the element of Water,
Bring peace upon my heart,
I call upon the element of Earth,
Strengthen my resolve.

Mabon

Aidan Kelly was a witch who gave the name Mabon to the Autumn Equinox. Mabon or Modron was a Welsh hero and means the son of the mother. Many witches don't use the term Mabon, they instead refer to it as the Autumnal Equinox. The name isn't important as it is the season and the energy of balance that influences us the most.

In the northern hemisphere Mabon falls between September 19th to 23rd and in the Southern hemisphere it falls between March 19th to 23rd. This is the time of year where the God begins to lose his power and decline. We begin to notice that the Sun is losing his energy and power and the weather is becoming cooler. Leaves fall from the trees and many animals begin to prepare for winter by storing food.

Libra brings a strong sense of balance to the northern hemisphere at this time while Aries brings some fire to the energy in the southern hemisphere.

Mabon is also the celebration of the reaping of the Second Harvest following Lughnasadh. The next and final harvest of the solar year is Samhain. While half the world is opening up to spring, bringing in new life and new creations, the other half of the planet is experiencing the opposite, becoming introverted and reaping what has been harvested. While one half is springing forth new growth, the other half is transforming and dying off. This polarity is balanced the further you get toward the equator.

At Mabon we take that which is no longer necessary and release it. It's the time to focus on shadow work. I'll talk more about shadow work in the next chapter.

It's also another opportunity to focus on gratitude for what you've reaped. Celebrate the changing of the seasons and feel into how this time of equal day and night is balanced.

You may find it very helpful to invest in a diary to help you record your experiences and activities during the sabbats. This can help you connect more deeply to your higher self, nature and spirit. You can use your diary to recall your progression throughout the year. You may find that much of what you discovered during various sabbats may have been forgotten.

Alongside a personal journal, Wiccans also keep what is called a "Book of Shadows" or BOS. This book contains all of our spells, rituals, herbal and crystal correspondences as well as various symbols used in the craft. Many witches keep a hand written book whilst others keep all of their work on their computer or store it in the cloud.

While it's traditional to have a hand written BOS, it's not necessary for the modern witch. A physical book will hold energy though. If you don't want to handwrite all of your work you can print out hard copies of your online documents and store them in a folder.

There are many beautiful BOS designs that you can buy online. Many witches make their own. It's really up to you as to how much money you spend and how creative you want to be. Some witches will organise their BOS into different sections. This does make it easier to reference, especially if you want to repeat spells and refer to lists or herbs and crystals.

The main sections you'll need in your BOS are: Rituals, Prayers and Chants, Deities, Spells, Correspondences, Oils and Potions, Magickal Alphabets and Meditations. You may find other topics to add to yours, the list above is just an example.

Once you have your book or folder you can consecrate it using the following rite.

Consecrating Your Book of Shadows

Light some frankincense or dragons blood incense. Take your book and move it slowly through the incense smoke. As you do say the following:

Lord and Lady of the Wicca,
Bear witness to my rite,
I consecrate this Book of Shadows, that it may be fit to serve
me in my work. Remove all malefic and replace with benefic.

See the smoke imbue your BOS with sacred smoke.

In the Mystery Witch School Academy, we blend our personal work with the ritual work we do with the deities during the sabbats. Working with the deities can help you gain more wisdom along the path. They are more than willing to help you discover who you truly are.

Even if you don't live in a climate that corresponds to the traditional sabbat imagery, work with what you do have. I live in a sub-tropical climate where we don't have much of a cold winter. Our trees are mostly evergreen and we don't experience much of that lovely colour palate of autumn.

I make the most of what I have where I live. I celebrate the changing temperatures and the way the sunlight becomes more mellow at winter time. I love how clear the ocean gets between Samhain and Imbolc. It's more still at this time. There is an energy of quietude at this time.

Whatever season it happens to be for you right now as you read this, what do you notice the most about it. How does nature change around you? What are your seasons?

Inner Shadow Work

Chapter Nine

The shadow was traditionally a term used by Jungian psychologists to refer to aspects of our personality and behaviour that we can't see or don't acknowledge. We are social creatures and to get by in communities we have to suppress and control various aspects of our behaviour and desires.

These aspects include our beliefs about ourselves and the world around us as well as personality traits that are socially deemed inappropriate or wrong. The shadow can also include the light shadow. These are positive qualities and talents we have but are too afraid to express due to self-doubt and fear.

It's called the shadow because it's hidden. It's hidden from ourselves mostly, our shadow qualities will reveal themselves to others, but we're usually in denial of them.

The ancient Egyptians believed that the Shadow was the fertile soil of creation. They believed that the shadow held spiritual solutions for living and for creativity. Being in the shadows didn't equate to evil, it simply couldn't be seen.

When we talk about doing shadow work, we are using processes of self-inquiry to shine a light on our personal shadow. Shining this light helps us see the truth of what makes us who we are. It's also the seat of our power.

Many Wiccan covens incorporate shadow work into their second degree training. My coven never did this but life certainly provided me with many opportunities to do this kind of work.

The shadow contains parts of ourselves that we've been told by our family, culture, schooling and religion aren't right or acceptable. As a result, when we experience these aspects of our personality, we either judge ourselves for having them or we deny they exist.

Most of us try really hard to act in ways that won't reveal these unacceptable parts of ourselves. Yet every human being on this planet has a shadow and we all share the same shadow qualities. No one is exempt from having a shadow and no one is exempt from having these qualities.

This may be a difficult pill to swallow. When we think of the most heinous of crimes, we think that we couldn't possible commit those ourselves. We all have these qualities in varying proportions. Some people are more narcistic than others while other people are greedier. It's all a matter of scale.

This doesn't mean that we all can become serial killers. Psychopaths are extreme cases and often have other factors contributing to their behaviour. When it comes to Wiccan shadow work, we're really just focusing on the general qualities that most people experience.

Shadow work demonstrates the hermetic principle of polarity. This principle states that some things in essence are the same they simply differ by degree. Hot and cold are in essence temperature but they vary in degree of warmth and coolness. When it comes to polarity one end can be transformed into its opposite because of the fact that they are the same in essence. When we change something that is hot to cold, we are changing the degree of temperature.

It's the same with our shadow qualities. Greed can turn into generosity and hatred can turn into love. Once we understand what is behind our more negative qualities, we can begin the journey toward turning them into something positive and useful.

Shadow work begins with the courageous decision to own our darker qualities. Once we acknowledge them, we can begin to transform them. If we don't then we will always remain unconscious to a large part of who we are.

Shadow work is important to do because our shadow qualities will always surface. Even if we aren't aware of them or don't wish to own them, they are there. When something is in the shadow it will come out when you least expect it to. This will often be out of your control because it's imbedded in your subconscious mind. When this happens it can ruin relationships, careers and communities.

The shadow can reveal itself through extreme arrogance, selfishness and narcissism. It can cause a person to think and behave in very callous and hurtful ways. When cultures share the same shadow qualities it can cause mass hysteria, division and genocide. We can see this in the witch trials during the 16th and 17th centuries. These mass murders were fuelled through propaganda, fear mongering and division.

During the witch trials the shadow qualities involved were fear, hatred, greed, desire for control and domination. As humans we are always susceptible to this mass indoctrination. We must always be on guard. That's why it's important for us to do our shadow work, because if we don't, we can fall prey to the mass shadow and get swept away in hysteria.

Our power is in our shadow and when we integrate it, we are able to be more authentic. Those shadow qualities that have been somewhat negative cease being negative and can actually empower us to become stronger and more emotionally balanced people. This allows us more control over our behaviour and reactions. We can stand back and look at ourselves before succumbing to fear, hatred, greed or power.

Once we integrate the shadow, qualities such as selfishness and arrogance can become self-care and confidence. Consequently, when we take care of ourselves, we're more open to helping and caring for other people. When we are confident, we can assertively maintain our boundaries and gain more respect. Being confident also allows us to be humbler because we no longer need to prove ourselves.

When doing shadow work, it's important not to be judgemental. Feeling guilt or shame isn't what you're trying to do. You can't shame yourself into changing the way you think unconsciously. It just suppresses the quality. Instead, you are exploring the qualities, owning them and then looking for the gift in them.

Initially the gift is in the opposite behaviour or quality. When you try to not be greedy you will deliberately try to share. When you are trying not to be arrogant you will be deliberately humbler. These are the polar opposite of the shadow quality.

What may come as a surprise is that there are gifts in the negative qualities themselves if you dare to do the work to find them.

When you shine a light on the shadow, you'll realise that the motivation under all of the shadow qualities is fear. Fear is the root of all evil. Fear is always underneath greed, selfishness arrogance and the desire for power over others. Fear is the root of hatred and fear will always be our downfall. Fear can destroy lives, communities and cultures.

While we do need fear to survive, we also need to develop an awareness of when the fear is based on truth and when it is based on lies. Most of the time that which we are afraid of isn't real. I'm sure you've heard the phrase fear is false evidence appearing real.

Fear keeps us alive so we do need it. Without fear we would be careless and endanger our health and wellbeing. It is a good idea to stay away from a lion's den, however, a lot of our fears are rooted in beliefs that simply aren't true or may have been true once but aren't any more.

Our shadow qualities are a part of our ego. They are there to keep us safe, but when we try to align with our higher selves and be happier in life, these ego safety qualities can sabotage our happiness, not to mention the negative effects they can have on other people.

Often, we overcompensate for our shadow urges by becoming the opposite of them. Many people become over generous because they don't want to appear greedy so they give everything away and end up with nothing. This generally leads to resentment and suffering. The need to constantly give in order to appear generous to yourself or others is a consequence of fear. It's the fear of what other people will think.

Shadow work is about putting our fears under the microscope and making peace with both ends of the polarity. One end is destitution from over giving and the other is hoarding from greed.

We are so dependent on being a part of a tribe or community that we will sacrifice ourselves to fit in. It's a survival trait. Humans survive better in groups. One of our major fears is to be ostracised from the group, cast out to fend for ourselves. This is why we allow ourselves to buy into harmful political and religious ideologies and narratives.

The place to start shadow work is to look at what the quality is protecting you from, for example, greed is protecting you from lack, which is essentially the fear of not having enough. To the ego it's better to take it all in case you need it, however, behaving in this way keeps you in a state of fear. Look instead to the gift in greed. It's simply making sure you have enough. Greedy people usually have more than enough yet they still fear scarcity.

It can also extend to a belief that if other people have more than you do, they may become more powerful than you and possibly destroy you. As you can see the shadow belief can be there to "protect" you from a number of things.

So, to summarise, there are always two gifts contained in the shadow. In the case of greed, one is to be aware of the importance of generosity and sharing and the other is making sure that you have what you need.

Once you deal with the fear behind greed, you'll find that you naturally become more generous. This new generosity isn't born from feeling fear or doing it because it's the "right" thing to do. It's coming from a real desire to be generous. This is how we develop a true conscience.

The gift of the shadow is to teach you give from the heart and receive with gratitude. No judgement either way. Shadow work helps you integrate extreme qualities into attitudes and behaviour that are more productive for you. This actually helps you achieve more happiness and peace of mind.

As I've stated before, in occult law we always try to balance polarities by introducing what we call a ternary or a third principle. This third element contains both essences of the polarities but neutralises them. In the case of greed, the third force or neutralising factor would be knowing when to give and knowing when to take what you need. Knowing when to say "yes" and knowing when to say "no".

In the past, it's been taught that to be "spiritual" you must oppress or suppress the shadow because it's evil and dangerous. Suppressing the shadow is just pretending it's not there. Suppression doesn't treat the negative aspects of these shadow qualities. All it does is lock them away.

Have you tried to hold a beach ball under the water? What happens when you let go? Of course, it bounces back out of the water. The same happens to the suppressed and denied shadow qualities. They get pressed down under the water of your subconscious and then you have a confrontation with somebody or something unsettling happens to you and then bang, out comes the shadow. The results are usually negative and sometimes devastating.

The problem with running away from our shadow is that we become more judgemental and even self-righteous. When we judge qualities within ourselves, we judge them in others too. If we are in denial of our shadow then we will be particularly judgemental and critical of other people. It's the very things we are judgemental of in others that we aren't acknowledging in ourselves.

One of the best ways to work with the shadow is to see what you really despise in other people. What pushes your buttons? What triggers you about other people? You may be looking in a mirror. This mirror may be one you don't want to look at, yet, you'll be faced with it over and over again until you do.

The Universe has a way of helping us do the work we came here to do. This means that it will periodically place people and situations before us to challenge us. If a certain type of person keeps showing up in your life, ask yourself, what can I learn from this person? What are they teaching me about myself?

When you find something offensive in another human being look for a time when you may have either thought about or actually have been like them. You may not have been exactly like them but they may be reflecting something similar in you.

For example, if arrogant people really irritate you ask yourself, when have I ever been arrogant? When do I think arrogantly? When have I either thought about or actively been arrogant? Is it possible that I could do this again in the future?

There may be a natural inclination to feel defeated if you find your arrogance. You may become very disappointed in yourself. You may be tempted to even beat yourself up. Don't. Just look for the gift in it. If arrogance really irks you, it may be possible that you show a humbler self to the world. You may be the kind of person to actually put yourself down in order to not appear arrogant. This isn't helpful to you or anyone else.

The gift in recognising the arrogance is to write down what you may be arrogant about. When you can say, "I can be arrogant" and not feel shame, the arrogance will turn into confidence. You'll cease to judge others who are arrogant and you'll stop putting yourself and others down. Facing your arrogant shadow will make you truly humble. You won't have to pretend anymore. Facing the shadow is a humbling experience. There's no way it can't be. When we acknowledge our dark personality qualities, we become humbled by the experience.

Of course, we can still recognise arrogance in others but it will no longer create fear in us. We won't feel triggered by them. We also stop judging others with disdain. We'll no longer succumb to self-righteousness or virtue signalling. This makes for a much more compassionate and happier existence. This doesn't mean that we let people get away with behaviours that are harmful, it just means that we won't be emotionally damaged by them.

Another tremendous benefit of shadow work is that you'll become much less triggered by other people and events. If somebody begins throwing insults your way or they call you names like greedy or selfish you won't be triggered. You will simply understand that those qualities do exist inside of you. If you are truly being selfish then you can acknowledge it and adjust your behaviour. If you are simply practicing self-care than you'll be aware of that too and not succumb to their attempted coercion.

Unfortunately, we learn to manipulate each other through shaming and labelling. We may call someone greedy because we want what they have. We may think they have too much and we're missing out. If you have integrated your shadow, you won't be guilty of these manipulative tactics. You will also be immune to them when other's try it on you. In the case of selfishness, you'll know that what appears to be selfishness to them is just you confidently practicing self-care, plus, the selfishness they're seeing is actually their own selfishness being reflected back at them.

Happiness comes when we can stop judging ourselves and consequently others. When we learn that we can actually take control of how we feel we become empowered. Shadow work enables us to have more dominion over our feelings and emotions. We stop blaming others for the way we feel and we naturally enjoy taking responsibility for our own condition.

In a world that encourages fear and victimhood, we become powerful. It's easy to blame others for the way we feel. It takes courage and work to take back our authority over ourselves. It takes guts because it's not easy.

We can also investigate our light shadow by observing the people we admire and like. These people will be mirroring our strengths and qualities that we value. When we look up to someone, we are really just seeing the qualities we have within ourselves that we don't believe we possess.

We can use the same processes to access these positive qualities within ourselves and learn to confidently express them.

Reprogramming the Ego

The shadow belongs to our ego. Our ego is a part of our consciousness that exists to keep us safe in this material existence. The ego dies not long after our body dies and we can't take either with us beyond death.

Children from the ages of 1 to 7 learn what is safe and what isn't. During those years we a are predominately in a theta brain wave state. This means that we were most suggestible between these ages. Many of our beliefs about ourselves and the world around us were created at this time.

Shadow work helps us reprogramme the ego so that it becomes a servant to the Higher Self. The ego is wonderful servant but a terrible master.

Our Higher Self is our True Self. It's our consciousness

that eternally exists. Some people call it the Atman, Spirit or Soul. This is who we truly are. This part of ourselves should be the one in control and not the ego. The problem is that our ego thinks it is the one in control and that it is the True Self.

When we say that we identify as someone or something it's the ego talking. The ego needs to identify to feel safe. It is a part of its function. Yet, in truth the things we identify with are as impermeant as our physical bodies are. We can't take them with us when we die.

Even though we need labels to help us communicate and understand the physical world, these labels can also be a hindrance. We need balance between being too identified and not acknowledging physical truths.

Shadow work for me has been about questioning the beliefs that I grew up with. The beliefs even within my own religious paradigm and finding out what is real and what isn't. There have been a lot of beliefs that I have had to change and let go of. So many of them prevented me from expressing my true Self and doing what I love doing and wanted to do. It wasn't an easy journey but well worth the time and effort.

Questioning your beliefs helps raise your consciousness. We have such wonderful techniques to help change the programming of the subconscious mind now. We are able to change our synaptic connections using energy psychology and gestalt processes.

If I hadn't done the shadow work, I would never have come out of the broom closet about being a witch. I wouldn't be writing this book or recording YouTube videos. I know that there are a lot of people who have so much to offer the world, yet are hindered from doing so due to beliefs about not being good enough in some way shape or form.

Shadow work can be very confrontational. You'll find that you'll be confronting aspects of yourself that contradict mainstream beliefs. You'll discover new aspects of yourself and your truth that will challenge your idea of what a "spiritual" person is or does.

However, it's worth the trip. You will see a bigger picture. You will be able to detach yourself from the fear mongering in the world. You won't get so caught up in the hype of what's going on in the world. You will be able to fly high like an eagle and see what is worth your concern and what isn't.

Shadow and Magick

If you find yourself consistently struggling with getting results from your magick, it may be time to actually look into the shadow. It's possible that your ego may be guarding you from something.

Do you have beliefs about yourself or the world that may not be true?

We spend a lot of energy trying to be what we think we should be to please friends, family, social groups, ideologies etc. Our shadow will reveal our true selves, we can't hide from it.

If you're casting a spell but feel guilty about having what you want because it will make you appear selfish then you're likely to sabotage the outcome. This can be one of the reasons why some spells don't work or only work temporarily.

If you have beliefs about money like, "spiritual people shouldn't want money" or "money is the root of all evil" then your money spells are probably not going to work very well.

These beliefs can stifle your magick from working both

energetically and practically. On an energetic level you are sending cross signals out into the world. You say you want money but your subconscious is saying you don't. You're practically cancelling the magick before it's had a chance to work.

More often than not, it's your behaviour that will interfere with the results of your magick. Your beliefs influence your actions so they may be preventing you from doing what you need to do to help the magick land.

A way to address this shadow block is to imagine that you have achieved your magickal results. Pretend that you are celebrating these results with your friends and family. Notice how they react in your imaginary scene. Some will be happy for you, but some may not be. It's not so much that it is those people who are hindering you, it's more likely that your perception of them and their potential judgement is what is inhibiting you. What you perceive from this visualisation is a picture of the various beliefs that you hold about yourself and the world.

The beliefs are generally centred around what other people will think of you or do to you if you achieve what you really want to achieve. These are the issues you need to work on.

Standing in your power is an ongoing process. It's like peeling an artichoke, there's always other layers underneath what you've already peeled off. It is about knowing who you are and knowing why you're here. If you truly want to create the life that you want to live then shadow work is essential.

We are creative beings and the shadow work helps us become more creative in a way that is more positive and more functional for us and others.

Shadow work is probably one of the most important

things you could probably ever do with your life and it's probably one of the most important aspects of spiritual practice as well. Rather than reacting to people and events in the same old automatic ways we can choose new behaviours which may bring us far better results. It is then that we realise how in changing ourselves we begin to change the world around us.

Sacred Dance and Voice

Chapter Ten

Many of the activities that we enjoy in our lives can be incorporated into our sacred practice. This is especially true of the arts.

My first love, when it comes to the arts, is dance. This is closely followed by singing and music. One of my favourite childhood performance spaces was a bank. Next to the entrance of the bank there was a large unused area with a marble background and pot plants, it was here that I would sing and dance to my heart's content while my mother waited outside the window for the bus. My 4-year-old imagination transformed that unused space into a grand stage.

We are artistic creatures and through the arts we can connect with ourselves, our practice and our magick.

Throughout history dance has played an important role in religious and magickal ritual. All cultures from around the world incorporate dance into their sacred ceremonies. Dances tell stories of people, culture and beliefs. Human interactions with the environment, gods and each other were and still are portrayed in dance.

Many dances are narratives that communicate messages from the gods and characters from various pantheons and epics. You'll see pictures of dancing figures on rocks, pots and frescos that are thousands of years old.

When dance is connecting with the deepest parts of ourselves, we are creating the sacred. Sacred dance doesn't have to be something you need to do in order to be changed by it. Watching others dance can have an equally profound effect on you.

We are designed to move. Everything moves. Everything vibrates. Dance is a way of flowing with the movement of life. Sacred dance can be as simple as a slow movement meditation or as powerful as brisk stomping and leaping to the sound of drumming.

It can be as simple or as complex as you want it to be. The important thing is to feel the connection of heart and soul to the experience of moving in a way that has meaning.

Dance is an art in real time and the experience is different every time you perform. Even if you're doing the same sequence over and over it will be slightly different each time to repeat it. It's the perfect metaphor for how life is constantly in a state of flux.

If you struggle with sitting meditation then dance may be the perfect option. It can be a somatic moving meditation where your mind becomes focused as you observe the way your body feels moving through space.

It can be a vehicle for exploring shadow work where you can give form to emotional sensations as you feel them in your body. This therapeutic use of dance can reveal where your limiting beliefs and thoughts are arising from. All you have to do is tune into where and how your body wants to move. You can also tune into your emotions and allow the movement to reveal their depth.

In this chapter, we'll be exploring how you can incorporate dance into your Wiccan practice. There is no need for you to have any dance experience. Whatever your preconceptions are about dance leave them at the door. Your dance is about your relationship to you and the gods.

Genres and Styles

My dance background is mostly in contemporary dance, ballet and some belly dancing. This background heavily influences the way I move. Movement is like a language, there is a vocabulary. This vocabulary is nuanced through your experiences of moving.

If you come from a martial arts background, you'll find your movement vocabulary will most likely be made up of various martial arts moves. If you have a belly dancing background then you'll have a lot of movement language centred around your hips and shoulders.

One of the benefits of having dance training is that it can provide you with a more extensive vocabulary so if you find that dance is something you want to explore then it's worthwhile taking some classes in whatever dance form appeals to you. However, it's not necessary.

While sacred dance is a genre of dance it isn't a style of dance. You can come from any dance background and still create sacred dances using whatever movement vocabulary you have. When you explore sacred dance from around the world, you'll find a lot of variation on movement styles, themes and vocabulary.

Some people combine dance styles with qi gong, tai chi and yoga. Many of the western chakra dancing and shakti dancing that you'll see are based around belly dancing and general rhythmic movement. The more you explore, the more movement language you will have to play with.

Warming Up

When you start your practice, you'll need to warm up

your body. This can be the perfect opportunity to work on your grounding and centring practice.

An easy way to begin is to stand with your feet shoulder width apart. Feel your feet connecting to the floor and imagine you have tree roots growing deep into the earth. You can breathe the energy of the earth up through these roots and circulate the energy throughout your entire body.

As you breath this energy up through your legs and spine feel how your body is coming alive with vibration. You can also gather energy into your body by moving your arms out to the side, over your head and then down in front of you as if you are gathering energy into your solar plexus.

This way you're connecting to the earth, the sky and your physical being all at the same time. Your body becomes the trunk of the sacred world tree. You become a conduit of divine energy.

Warming up should ensure that you are moving your body in a way that starts out as moderate, slowly getting the blood flowing into your muscles and gently mobilising your limbs, back, neck and shoulders. You know your body and what its limitations are so make sure you are gentle with it.

When it comes to beginning your dance ritual, start with exploration first. You can spend time just learning how your body likes to move by putting on some music and going with the flow. You don't need to have any purpose other than to explore what it feels like to move. Discover the joy of moving.

There are many devices that you can use to explore sacred dance more fully like playing with weight, space, breath and energy, but start with just feeling the joy. Even if you feel stiff and uncoordinated, allow yourself to move through the space without judgement or criticism.

Dancing the Four Elements

Using dance to help you connect to the four elements is a great place to start your journey into sacred dance.

Water

Imagine that you are a sea spirit or ocean deity. What would it feel like if the space around you was actually water? How does your body move when it's moving through water? Allow your hands to move back and forth through this water. Connect with the feeling of the element of water – cold and moist.

If you struggle with kinetic imagination, try filling a basin or bath and run your hands through the water. Get used to the feeling of moving through water.

The movement will be fairly slow as you have to press against the weight of the water.

How does the element of water inspire you to move? Water can be gentle, flowing or it can be rough and tumultuous. How does it feel to be moved by the element of water?

You can extend this feeling to imagine that you are water. How does being water inform your dance? Does it change how you move? Are you discovering new movements you've never done before?

As I dance through the water, I feel it's gentle weight. The space is denser and I find that I have to push slightly as I move my body through it.

When I am water, I feel loose. I feel the fluidity. I even notice that my muscles begin to relax more.

Fire

When exploring the element of fire focus on the warmth. How can your body be like fire? Fire shakes and shimmers, it crackles. Yet a flame can also stand tall and still.

As I dance the dance of the flame, I feel the warmth in my body. I feel energised by the heat and can direct its energy through my arms and feet out into the world. Through the element of fire, I can set up a fire ring as my sacred circle simply through projecting it out. Of course, once this is done with, I extinguish the flames via the element of water.

Air

The element of air is lighter than that of water. As you dance through the air notice how easy it is to move through it. Can the element of air lift you up? Does moving through it allow you to breathe more easily?

As you become the element of air you may feel like running and leaping. You may find yourself rising onto your toes as if you could just fly away.

Dancing the air dance encourages me to extend my limbs out into the space. I find myself taking up more space as I move through it. When I connect to the element of air within myself it lightens my load. I can feel supported by the air as I balance and fall, letting go of the need for control.

Earth

The element of earth can feel quite dense. It can be solid to move through. More effort may be needed. How does the resistance of the weight of earth inform how you move? How does the earthy texture feel on your body?

As you feel the element of earth within you, how does it ground you? Do you feel yourself becoming more connected to the earth as you move? Does the earth encourage you to move into the floor and connect more with the ground beneath you?

There is a sense of moving through more resistance which allows for slower and more considered movement. I feel the weight of my own body sinking into the earth. I find myself sometimes just rolling along the floor feeling my whole body sinking into it.

Dancing to Raise Energy for Spell Casting

Focusing on your movement can help you connect more with your magical intent energetically and emotionally. We feel emotion in our bodies. Without a body we couldn't experience emotion at all.

The next time you feel an emotion, take notice of where you're experiencing it in your body. If you were to dance that emotion, how would your body move?

Dance can be abstract or it can be a narrative. You can tell the story of your intent, acting it out through movement or you can simply move to the rhythm of your spell chant.

As you visualise your intent notice how you feel in your body. When you allow yourself to follow the movement impulse you may be surprised at what movement you experience.

The more connected you are to your body, the easier it is to connect with your inner being. The body has long been diminished by many spiritual traditions, yet, the way to liberate our spiritual nature in this life is through the body.

The body has its own intelligence. This intelligence transcends our intellect and head knowledge. Our intuition is experienced through our body. We often experience feelings in our gut when our intuition is trying to warn us about possible danger. If we are trying to make a decision, simply placing our hand over our heart chakra can help us intuit the right course of action to take. Our body is a scared instrument through which our divine self gets to experience the world of physical existence.

The time to incorporate dance into your magick would be when you begin to chant your spell. Voice and movement are all about vibration, so as you're chanting your spell you can dance your desire into being.

As you are dancing you can be focused on your intent or simply on the chant. Focus on gathering the energy and sending it out. Gather the energy by sweeping your arms up over your head and bringing them into the centre of your body and then push the energy away out into the world through pushing gestures.

Don't be afraid of using your whole body in the process.

Dancing in Ritual

Dance has been incorporated into sacred rites for thousands of years. Many rites from ancient people included music, chanting and dancing.

Dancing can tell a story of the battle between the Oak and Holly King. Through dance you can welcome in the spring. You can dance while chanting to the Goddess and God.

The very act of drawing down the moon can be danced as the lunar energies are embodied through movement. Your dance can be offered up as a prayer or libation to the gods during a ritual or after spell casting. A simple movement sequence can be a part of your daily practice as you ground and centre your energy and then invoke the Goddess and God.

You sacred circle can be your space to dance as you connect with your spiritual self, the earth and the gods.

Dancing for Healing

Dance is often used to facilitate emotional healing. Many popular dance forms like chakra dance and tantric dancing can assist the dancer to heal traumas and express emotional impulses.

Dance can be very therapeutic. Any of the arts can be used as a form of release therapy. If you do find yourself needing to touch base with how you feel or even express how you feel in a safe way, then dance can be the perfect medium.

Dance can help you uncover hidden sadness, grief and anger. It can also help you transform these feelings into hope, acceptance and joy. Sometimes the subconscious mind just wants you to acknowledge your fears and sadness in order for you to heal and move on. Dance can be the perfect modality to help you transform emotional energy.

The way we move and hold ourselves affects how we feel. We can change how we feel simply by changing our posture. Take notice of how you sit when you are feeling self-doubt. You'll notice that the chest is curved inward and your shoulders may also be rounded forward.

You can change your posture to mimic the posture of confidence simply by pulling the shoulders gently down and back and holding your chest open.

This way dance can be used to help you change how your feel. The next time you're feeling down try dancing in a joyful way for one to two minutes. How do you feel after a few minutes of dancing this way?

You can do the same with a simple posture. Try forming a posture in a way that mimics joy. Hold it for three to five minutes. How do you feel?

Meditation

There are a lot of people who struggle to meditate. It isn't easy to sit for ten to thirty minutes without moving while trying to focus the mind on one thing. As an alternative, many people prefer to do yoga, qi gong or tai chi. These slow movement styles can help calm the mind and improve your concentration.

Concentration brings the mind home to stillness and tranquillity. When you are focused on a movement sequence you let go of all worries and thoughts that would normally compete for your mind's attention.

When doing dance as a form of meditation, focus on slow movement. Feel into the sensation of the movement itself. Observe the movement as you dance it. Feel the space around you as you move through it. Feel the movement being initiated from your solar plexus so that your limbs feel more connected to your centre. You aren't just an arm or a leg, your whole body is involved in the movement even if you're only moving your hand.

Using dance as a meditation helps you feel more connected to your own body. It helps you become more aware of yourself and can take you into the realm of discovering your true self underneath the restrictions and camouflage of the ego.

Your Magical Voice

Your voice is powerful. In magick we call a powerful and commanding voice your "magickal" voice. Many ceremonial magicians cultivate this voice of authority.

The voice is the carrier of vibration. What you say has power especially when you are focused on your intention. The word spell comes from the word spelling. To spell something is to vocalise your magick.

When you chant your spells, you are sending your intent out into the world through vibration. When you're commanding vibration matches the energy of your intent, you should feel aligned to your magical ability.

Like dance, your voice can change how you feel. Try saying "I am good enough" with your shoulders rounded and head facing downwards. What do you feel in your throat and how does the voice sound when you do this?

Now, take the posture of someone who is confident. Say, "I am good enough". How has the voice changed? How do you feel emotionally? You can use this technique in your magick. Whenever you cast a spell make sure you are in a confident posture and your vibration will be stronger.

You can chant your spell many times until you really feel it's time to stop. Sometimes, just rehearsing the spell can begin the magical process. If you say the spell with authority and conviction you may just get the result before you've lit the candle.

Your magickal voice must be commanding. It doesn't have to be loud and forceful, just assertive and assured. Many people lower their voice for this but you can experiment with pitch and tone. Remember, it's how the voice makes you feel that will be the indicator that you have it right. If your voice instils a feeling of confidence and certainty then you're on the right path.

Your voice can also be used in ritual to connect you to a deity. Many cultures use mantra to connect and invoke deities. One of the deities I've worked with for a long time is the Buddhist goddess, Tara. She has different mantras depending on which aspect I'm working with.

You can use the IO EVOHE mantra which is very common in Wicca. The IO is a seed syllable for the goddess Isis and the Evo He is used for Dionysius or Bacchus. This chant is a chant of the ecstasy of creation and the blending of masculine and feminine creative energies. Perfect for magick.

If you are working with deities who don't have known mantras, you can make up your own mantra through using their name and putting an IO in front of it.

Mantras are usually seed syllables that relate to qualities of the God or Goddess. They aren't sentences or phrases. In the west we'll often construct a short phrase to use as a mantra but these aren't true mantras.

The power of the mantra is in the vibration of the seed syllables. You don't need to know what they mean, it's the flow and rhythm that connect you with the deity.

Of course, you can combine the voice work with your dance to raise energy, connect with deities and enjoy yourself in the process.

Any of the arts can be incorporated into your witchcraft practice. Your paintings can be talismans. Your sculptures can be deities. You can use music to compose rituals songs and musical spells. The craft of the wise can be expressed and practiced through many creative practices.

Witchcraft is an art and a craft. You don't have to limit yourself to traditional styles of magick like candle magick, use your creativity, incorporate your skills with your intentions and you will discover many ways to practice your craft.

Self Initiation and Advancing Your Practice

Chapter Eleven

Human beings are a social species and we learn from each other. The stories, the mistakes and the triumphs of other people can show us what works and what doesn't. Traditionally, witchcraft, shamanism and all magical practices were taught one to one, however, teaching one to one these days can be difficult as it takes time. One person can't spend the amount of time required with many students one to one. Fortunately, witchcraft can be taught in groups.

Books are great resources to introduce us to new ideas, concepts and processes but they don't actually teach us anything. All we get from reading a book is intellectual knowledge. Until we put that knowledge into a regular practice, we learn nothing.

Real learning derives from experience, examples from others and person to person conversation. There is a transmission of teachings and energy that comes from learning directly from a person that is rarely achieved from reading a book. Watching someone, listening to them and being able to ask questions is key to learning, especially when it comes to the mystical and the magical.

When we are on our own it's easy for the ego to think it knows best. We can fool ourselves into thinking we know more than we do. Being in a group or working with someone can humble the ego so we can open the way to really learning something new. It's very easy to get comfortable with our own routines. When we start learning from someone else, they will introduce us to new practices which may challenge us in many ways.

Nothing is gained in magick without effort and self-discipline. It's not easy to walk this path alone. This is why covens can be so useful. Even if witches of the past didn't work in covens as we do today, the coven is a valuable learning environment. You get to connect with others and form a tight community of beings who have similar goals and aspirations.

Covens are like a family. They are tight. The sharing of experiences in ritual brings individuals together as a community celebrating the challenges and joys of life. Coven members watch out for each other, help each out and learn and grow together, however, it's not always possible to find a coven.

Covens vary in their focus too. The leadership of the coven is important and the way a coven is structured doesn't suit everyone. Wherever groups of people gather there are also groups of egos gathering there as well. Not all egos get on or agree on things.

Solitary practice is often a solution for many Wiccans. Being a solitary doesn't mean you never attend gatherings or rites with others. When I was in my covens, we often had public rituals where solitaries would come and celebrate the sabbats with us. We went to pagan gatherings with both covens and solitaries.

In modern times we are fortunate to have the internet.

This gives us the ability to connect with withes from all over the globe. The Mystery Witch School community is such a group. In the Academy we meet online twice a month to celebrate the New and Full Moons. We have members who are in the USA, Canada, Australia, the UK, Europe and India. There are no boundaries. Witches are resourceful people, we make do with what we have and if we can create something better, we will do just that.

Traditional covens are usually structured in a hierarchical fashion. This is mostly because they are influenced by free masonry and ceremonial magickal orders. The level of attainment called a degree is celebrated via various initiations.

A lot of modern covens don't use the degree system and instead may only have one initiation.

Initiation simply means to begin something. It's the way to formalise a beginning or to celebrate stepping into something new and different. It signifies that a change has occurred.

Traditionally, to achieve the next level of initiation in Wicca a person would have to go through what is called an "ordeal". This is a test of some kind. Sometimes it's a test of psychic ability or knowledge, you may be asked to read an object that belongs to someone using the skill called psychometry. Another test may be to do an astrological chart for someone. Popular first-degree initiations require the candidate to spend a whole night in a forest by themselves with nothing other than the cloths they are wearing and a bottle of water. These ordeals aren't dangerous or painful, they are just challenging in mild ways.

It is traditional in Wicca for the initiate to pass through three degrees. Once the third degree is achieved, they would then hive off and form a new coven.

Why Initiation?

Initiations are common in most mystical and magickal traditions around the world. Even in the shamanic lineage you will find the practice of initiation. Some traditional initiations are incredibly challenging and even frightening. They can make Wiccan initiations seem like kindergarten play.

When it comes to traditional Wiccan initiations, the candidate is initiated by someone who has also been previously initiated. You would be able to follow the lineage of initiators back to people like Gerald Gardner for example. He was also initiated by someone who had been initiated so we don't know how far back his lineage goes.

Many witches and occultists have had numerous teachers. When you're initiated by them you are energetically connecting to their lineage. When you're learning from someone either in a coven, privately or in an online group you are receiving the teachings and energy of their lineage.

What you're receiving is all of the history energetically of all of the people who've ever been involved in that tradition. The Sufis say that you're also getting the protection of that lineage as well and all of those who have passed who have participated in that lineage. This energetic transmission is practiced all around the world in mysticism, magick and religion.

In modern times, it may not be as common to be initiated by someone who has a lineage. Many covens are formed by people who have never been in a coven prior to starting their own. The concept of a lineage may not be something many people know or care about. It's often debated. Some people believe that a lineage is necessary while other don't.

When you're a solitary and self-initiating either by choice or circumstance, it's pretty much between you and the gods. There is no direct lineage or transmission from another person unless you have worked with them.

In this day and age, we can still pick up people's energy online but if you don't have access to any of that then you are truly in that self-initiation zone.

The self-initiation is where you make that statement of choice to follow the Wiccan or witchcraft path. You formally set up a ritual and state your intention. It is between you and the Divine and your Higher Self. Any initiation is between you, your Higher Self and the gods regardless of whether you're initiating into a coven or going it alone. The only difference is that you aren't adding the extra coven or group lineage to your tool kit.

In many ways initiation is something that has already happened to you when you start walking the magical path whether you're consciously aware of it or not. It's not really a choice. Usually, by the time you are ready for a "real world" initiation you've already reached the new stage energetically. The ritual is just a way of acknowledging it on the material plane.

You can't force an initiation before it's time either. A ceremony doesn't actually initiate. It's the work you do leading up to the ceremony that prepares you. In many ways life is full of initiations. Each challenge you face in life that you manage to triumph over is an initiation of some kind.

At the end of the day, your goal is to find your inner guru, your true self who can guide you on the path. Being initiated through another person is really just at the beginning stages.

Initiation comes out of a dedication to your path. Some

people will do a self-dedication first as a statement that this is their commitment to themselves. They will ritually state that they will dedicate time and energy to learning and walking the Wiccan path.

Often the first imitation will occur after a year of formal practice. I provide members of the Mystery Witch School Academy with a self-initiation ceremony at the end of the 12-month course. Some people take longer than 12 months and that's fine. People work within their own timeframe. The school is a blend of solitary study and group learning. The transmission is from me to the students. The initiation ceremony is really just a formalisation of what has already occurred.

Not everyone will be in a place of initiation after 12 months of study. It takes more than knowledge to truly be initiated. Something inside of you has to evolve and grow as well. Take your time. You don't need to accumulate degrees and formal levels of initiations. In the spiritual world head knowledge doesn't mean a thing. Allow the organic initiation to happen to you and then celebrate it with a ritual once you feel it's time.

Instead of rushing to do an initiation ceremony it's more advisable to start with a self-dedication rite. A self-dedication is an announcement to yourself and the gods that you are ready to walk the Wiccan path. You can do this dedication soon after you start practicing Wicca.

It's an acknowledgement of your commitment to you and your spiritual growth. In many ways this is like an initiation. You are initiating a new lifestyle incorporating daily practices and rites into your life in order to experience a deeper meaning in life. This dedication is just as important as any initiation ceremony. It marks your readiness to sacrifice your time and energy to find more joy and connection in your life.

Self-Dedication Rite

You can do a simple self-dedication by going some-where in nature and doing a small ceremony. Cast your circle, invoke the Goddess and God and then say the fol-lowing:

>*At this time and in the place, I stand before the Goddess and God of the Wicca,*
>
>*I stand as one with all of nature and I honour the life contained within all things,*
>
>*From this day forth I walk the Wiccan Path and Strive to learn the ways of old,*
>
>*I strive to honour the Earth and all her beings,*
>
>*I strive to learn about myself and express my highest self in the world.*

Spend some time contemplating what this means and see yourself incorporating your witchcraft practice into your daily life.

Advancing Your Studies

Many people come to the craft in order to acquire psy-chic powers and supernatural abilities. Although having these skills may seem like they will give you more control or power, they really aren't the answer to happiness or joyful living.

Skills like divination, reading auras, psychometry, as-tral travelling, communicating with spirits and learning advanced magickal techniques are very useful. They can help you gather more information, help you with deci-sion making and bring good things into your life.

However, they aren't where the real power lies. The real power comes from your true self knowledge and aware-ess of who and what you really are. It's often the ego that wants all of the powers and abilities. This is usually due to a feeling of disempowerment.

I have met witches who are very proud of being 3rd degree Gardnerian High Priestesses but their personal lives and psyche are a mess. They may well see auras and be able to read the tarot in their sleep but it hasn't really added any joy to their lives.

The work of inner enquiry and shadow work are really where the power comes from. This type of work begins with the ability to be able to quiet the mind and become more objective toward yourself and the world around you.

If you only ever do one practice on the path then make that practice be meditation. It may not sound as exciting as communicating with spirits or becoming a master magician but it will help you develop the ability to connect with yourself as well as other non-physical beings if that is your wish.

Right from the get go of your daily practice you should be incorporating meditation. Then when you're ready to learn divination and various other practices, you will be hopefully more balanced and less ego driven.

Sometimes these "powers" can be an ego trap. Without the grounding of self-knowledge and control over the ego, it's easy to fall into a false sense of spiritual attainment simply because you're more psychic.

Keeping all of this in mind, there will be a time when you'll want to develop your skills in divination, energy work, magick and dream interpretation etc.

Traditionally, in second degree we would be introduced to the various skills of a witch. These subjects of learning would be herbalism, divination, mediumship, astral travelling and astrology.

Any one of these subjects can take years to become proficient at. Many witches find that they are drawn to some practices and not others. We can't all be good at everything.

Some witches choose divination as their forte, often incorporating tarot with scrying and runes. Other witches will excel in astrology while some become great mediums. Many have more than one specialty.

As you progress along the path, you'll no doubt experiment with various advanced disciplines. Some you will connect with and desire to explore while others won't be of interest to you. You'll find that you may be great at working with the runes but lousy with scrying. You might find it really difficult to see auras but be great at magick and spell crafting.

You don't have to be good at everything a witch is supposed to be good at. You'll need to find your talents and learn to accept the things you're not good at. That's ok. You don't have to be super witch. At the end of the day, it's your connection to the gods and to yourself that will bring you the meaning and joy you're looking for and not the special skills that you may acquire along the way.

Take your time exploring and learning the craft. There is no finish line. The Craft of the Wise is an ongoing path full of new experiences and knowledge. You don't need to be in a rush to acquire massive amounts of occult knowledge in order to live a happy and joyful life. The most important thing is that you learn to craft a sacred pathway in which to walk as you journey through this miracle called life.

Reference List

Braden, G (2014) Resilience from The Heart, Hay House Australia Pty Ltd, Australia

Clark, R (2012) The Sacred Magic of Ancient Egypt, Llewellyn Publications, USA

Cunningham, S (1988) The Truth About Witchcraft Today, Llewellyn Publications, USA

Davis, M, From Man to Witch, Gerald Gardner 1946–1949, www.geraldgardner.com

Ford, D (1998) The Dark Side of the Light Chasers, Hodder and Stoughton, London

Glass, J (1974) Witchcraft and the Sixth Sense, Wilshire Book Co. USA

Hardy M (Editor) (2019) Ascendent: Modern Essays on Polytheism and Theology, Bibliotheca Alesandrina
Hutton, R (1999) Triumph of the moon, Oxford University Press, USA

Illes, J (2004) The Element Encyclopedia of 5000 Spells, HarperElement, London

Inman, S (2020) Tapping Into Abundance: Using EFT Tapping and Law of Attraction to Change Your Mindset and Turn Your Life Around, Sandra Inman Publishing, Australia.

Levi, E (1995) Transcendental Magic: It's Doctrine and Ritual, Bracken Books, London

Miller, J (2009) The Sorcerer's Secrets, The Career Press, USA

Penczak C (2003) The Inner Temple of Witchcraft, Llewellyn Publications, USA

Sadhu, M (1990) The Tarot, Unwin Hyman Limited, London

Three Initiates (1908), The Kybalion: A Study of The Hermetic Principles of Ancient Egypt and Greece, The Yogi Publication Society, Masonic Temple, Chicago.

About the Author

Sandra Inman has been empowering witches to confidently create a spiritual practice that connects them to their full potential, nature and the Universe for the past 8 years. She had been a Wiccan for almost 30 years and during this time she has also studied with various teachers from many spiritual traditions, Wiccan and non-Wiccan.

She is the founder of Mystery Witch School, where witches from all around the globe join together to practice the age-old craft. Sandra is also an EFT Tapping practitioner helping creative pagans tap into their strengths and remove psychological blocks that are preventing them from fully expressing their true selves in the world.

Sandra has an extensive background in the performing arts as a dancer, choreographer and singer and now hosts a YouTube channel revealing all things Wiccan and Witchcraft.

You can find out more about what the Mystery Witch School can offer you by going to:

Website:
 https://mysterywitchschool.coachesconsole.com/
Mystical Witch School YouTube Channel:
https://www.youtube.com/c/MysticalWitchSchool
Facebook: https://www.facebook.com/mysticalwicca

Free Resources

The 3 Vital Ingredients Successful Witches Use to Learn and Grow Their Wiccan Practice!

I'll let you in on a secret... There are 3 things that need to be sorted before starting any spiritual practice.

To find out more: https://tinyurl.com/3WiccanPrac

How to Start Your Witchcraft Practice

Here's The Beginner-Friendly Roadmap To Practising Wicca and Witchcraft!

A FREE 20-minute video that shows you exactly where to start learning and what you need to do to practice modern witchcraft easily and safely. You can access it here: https://tinyurl.com/startwitchvideo

How To Prepare for Successful Spellcasting!

Get on top of your spell casting with this simple checklist: Download it here: https://tinyurl.com/spellcasterchecklist

Mystery Witch Schoool 101 Academy

The Beginner-Friendly Way to Start Learning and Practising Wicca

Do you want to learn how to be a witch and be part of a community of like-minded people without the frustration of not knowing where to start or what to do?

The Mystery Witch School 101 Academy is aimed at witches who want to learn more about the craft, develop a deep connection to nature and themselves through regular online monthly lessons, mentoring and group support.

Start learning Wicca NOW! by clicking on the link below:

https://tinyurl.com/LearnWicca101

5 Days To A Wiccan Practice

Easy Online Video Course

Do you want to start a Daily Wiccan Practice
but don't know where to begin?

Do you hesitate to create a daily practice because you
don't feel you have enough time or the correct tools?

Over a 5 day period, I take you step-by-step through
a simple process that you can do every day to get you
started on the path of the witch.
Begin with a simple daily practice that you can do anywhere, at any time without needing anything other than
yourself!

**The Ultimate Guide to Starting a Wiccan Practice that
Works** 5-day online video course is the perfect place to
begin.

Start Today: https://tinyurl.com/DailyWiccan

Books By This Author

Tapping Into Abundance: Using Eft Tapping And Law Of Attraction The Change Your Mindset And Turn Your Life Around

If you want the Law Of Attraction to work for you without all of those limiting beliefs holding you back then keep reading...

Are you trying to manifest more money, a better career or love relationships into your life but can't get past what seems to be an invisible wall of resistance?

If so, you're not alone. In fact, most people who try to bring the principles of co-creation and manifestation into their lives struggle to make it happen. And if you're like most of them, you've tried all the normal mindset "hacks and re-frames": affirmations, positive thinking and creative visualisation. While these all have a place in manifestation, they have fallen short in dealing with the main cause of most of your failures.

So, what can you do about it all?

In Tapping Into Abundance: How to use EFT Tapping With The Law of Attraction to Change Your Mindset and Turn Your Life Around, Sandra Inman presents a very simple process. She guides you through a step-by-step program that teaches you how to use EFT (Emotional Freedom Technique) or Tapping, to release and eliminate limiting mindset blocks once and for all.

Looking at how your beliefs affect your behaviour and the quantum research surrounding energy and emotions Sandra opens your eyes to just how transformative tapping can be. She then provides you with processes that can lead to real change.

Sandra takes you on a journey that begins with what you want to manifest into your life right now. She teaches you how to use tapping to address the limiting beliefs and emotional discomfort that come up for you when you think about your dreams, goals and desires. As the journey continues, she helps you move to the deeper issues that created that invisible wall of resistance in the first place.

With easy-to-follow exercises and tapping scripts, Sandra helps you break down the walls of emotional pain and the underlying beliefs and vows that are causing this pain. She also addresses key blockages that you may not think you have.

Printed in Great Britain
by Amazon